A Teen's Guide to Critical Thinking

Protect Yourself from Phone and Social Media Addiction

ED WONNS

ED WONNS

ISBN: 979-8-9991576-0-7 (print)
ISBN: 979-8-9991576-1-4 (ebook)

ED WONNS

Table of Contents

ED WONNS

Introduction

This book is written for an audience of teens, aged from thirteen to nineteen by definition, however its contents may very well be addressed to a wider audience including older people, specifically parents.

The idea behind this book is to raise awareness over how a massive amount of information, through the internet, social media, the school system, the news, the groups one belongs to, isn't in most cases generated with the intent of helping individuals to think freely. Quite the opposite, in most cases its nature is manipulative and needs to be seriously addressed in order to save the freedom and dignity of each individual.

This book is structured as a dialogue between a parent (**P.**) and the parent's child (**C.**). The parent acts essentially as a tutor providing guidance to the child over how to develop critical thinking against being manipulated by the world surrounding the child.

Considering how today's teens are enveloped in a technological environment and how much of their social and intellective life takes place through the internet, they are heavily exposed to this environment without the appropriate defenses they should have.

The subtitle of this book explicitly declares the intent to protect against phone and social media addiction, so one may question why this specific matter is left to the final chapters of the book and isn't dealt with until beyond the first seven chapters.

The reason is that the first seven chapters are a necessary preparation for the following chapters which are dedicated to phones and social media. The objective is to create a solid foundation of critical thinking which is required in first place, before any interaction with phones and social media is taken into consideration.

It is worthwhile noting that the term "phone" is used here as a synonym of "smartphone", meaning a mobile handheld phone with computer-like functions, a touchscreen, and capable of browsing the web. The term "smartphone" is also used in the book when it has to be differentiated from the notion of a traditional phone which has no such features.

What Is Critical Thinking?

P. Today, I'll talk to you about what I believe is the most important quality a person should have. Some say the most important quality is to be good to others or to sacrifice yourself for others. This is what religions tell you. I will not dispute the importance of being good to others, but my take on the best you can be for yourself is to use critical thinking. We'll then see how this will impact the people around you as well.

C. What do you mean? The most important quality I should have is about criticizing? And, if so, criticize what?

P. It's actually quite the opposite of what you would be inclined to guess. Like many other English words, the word "critical" has its roots in ancient Greek, it derives from "krinein", which means "to judge" or "to express an opinion". Even if this may entail criticizing something, it can also entail its contrary, as a judgement can be either positive or negative. Now, in order to express an opinion on something, you must first understand it.

C. It's not about criticizing upfront, but all about understanding?

P. Yes, but there's something very very special about this way of understanding which differentiates it from other forms of understanding. When you think critically, you form your own view on any matter without letting yourself get influenced by anything else. Whether it's something you see, hear or read from anything or anyone, you rely on your own power of understanding things and nobody else's. Critical thinking empowers yourself as an individual.

C. What if I don't have enough power to understand things myself?

P. Don't be so hard on yourself. I will show you how you will learn to exert yourself to understand things at your best, always making sure you're not adopting ideas from someone or something which you haven't first verified in depth. Relying on other people's ideas without having first verified them yourself is defined as an uncritical stance, the opposite of critical thinking. If you go down the uncritical path like many people do, you will lose your individual self, and you will end up like a grain of sand on a beach, indistinguishable from other grains. Or like one of many sheep in a herd, taken over by what I call the sheep-effect.

C. What's the sheep-effect?

P. It's a condition by which individuals think according to the group they are part of, therefore sacrificing their own view in favor of the views of the group. They think like an extension of the group rather than thinking by themselves as individuals.

C. Why would they do that?

P. For many reasons, depending on case-by-case. They may simply be lazy, not wanting to investigate what caused certain events and therefore choose an easy explanation which is the one adopted by their group. Or they may be biased, sharing certain convictions which they want to stick to, so they dismiss considering any facts which can prove they are wrong. Or they may simply find it's easier to avoid asking too many questions.

C. You're saying people escape the truth?

P. Very much so. If you exercise critical thinking, you aspire to understand the truth, and this requires effort.

C. You want to teach me how to make use of critical thinking in order to understand the truth?

P. Understanding the truth is a big statement because we have limitations as human beings. There are cases when we may not be able to understand the truth, so what matters is to put your best efforts in trying to understand it. You need to find your own way without approving upfront what others tell you is the truth.

C. If you as a parent tell me as a child that you alone know the truth, and you set orders for me to follow, I can dispute what you're telling me and refuse to follow your orders, right?

P. Yes, provided you make use of your critical thinking to prove my orders are wrong. When you refuse to do something I'm requesting you to do, you must provide an explanation for it. Simply saying "I don't want to do it" isn't enough because you aren't providing thoughtful reasons for your refusal.

C. How about if I provide those thoughtful reasons, will you change your idea and your orders?

P. Yes, if your reasons are well explained and justified. If the power of your reasons overwhelms the reasons of my orders, then I should admit you're more right than myself, and I should therefore change my orders.

C. All the children in the world could unite and find ways to refuse taking orders from their parents.

P. You're scaring me. Your statement sounds similar to the political slogan of Karl Marx in his Manifesto of the Communist Party, first published in 1848, where he incited the workers of all countries to unite. As you may know, Marx was the ideological father of communism, a political movement which is well known for having generated horrible dictatorships and social catastrophes.

At any rate, I want to take you at face value and dig deeper into the matter. The time we're living allows ideas generated by society to go against traditional ideas which were nurtured within the family. The authority of the family or of your parents, is questioned by ideas which develop outside of the family. These ideas may find appeal in today's youth, potentially triggering your extreme statement about all the children in the world revolting against their parents.

The main point is to figure out whether those ideas which are generated outside of the family are critically analyzed by those children who refuse to follow orders from their parents, or whether those same children are useful idiots manipulated by certain forces within society which instill in them certain ideas.

C. I'm confused. You told me I could refuse to take orders from my parents, and then you're telling me I shouldn't because I may be a useful idiot manipulated by some force outside of my family.

P. Let me clarify. You must never lose your critical thinking, which never accepts as good any idea, regardless from where it comes, unless it's deeply thought over.

I'll explain it in a practical way. It would be wrong for me to say: "I'm your parent, therefore you must do this! Period!". When a parent sets orders without explaining the reasons for those orders, expecting the child to automatically execute them, that parent is killing her child's critical thinking, by assuming the child has to execute and never question. The argument according to which you have to do what I say, simply because I'm your parent, is typical of a military environment where orders have to be executed, no matter what. In that situation, who receives orders is deprived of her thinking capacity. Within that scenario, is the child considered as a thinking individual? Of course not.

C. You're confirming every order from a parent is up for debate.

P. In principle, yes. However, a good parent tries to understand the best option for her child and explains it. A good parent listens to the reasons of her child and explains why the child's reasons are wrong or right.

C. What about if the child doesn't agree?

P. The parent will have the right to impose her choice when the parent proves it's the most reasonable one for the child. However, this matter isn't just about your relationship to your parent, it has far wider relevance, it also has to do with your relations outside of your family.

C. What do you mean?

P. My point is that using critical thinking is something which has to drive your actions, no matter where you are. During the last century, parental authority has been gradually taken over by society, let's call it the "outside world", as opposed to the "inside world" of the family.
This is what concerns me the most. I want you to make use of critical thinking to protect yourself from anyone or anything who is trying to control your actions against your well-being. We considered your position within your family. However, unless you are a child so

unlucky to have parents who aren't respectful of you and don't care about your well-being, in most cases the threats to your freedom from the outside world are far greater.

C. Threats to my freedom from the outside world? What do you mean?

P. What I mean is that the outside world can be far more dangerous to your freedom of thought than your own family.

When your parents tell you what they think about events or situations, they usually tell you in a clear way what you should do or not do. Some easy examples: "do your homework", "it's late, time for bed", "brush your teeth", etc. However, the outside world is everything you interact with outside of your family, call it what you see on a smartphone, on social media, what friends around you are doing and saying, etc.

C. What's so dangerous about the outside world?

P. The danger is in the many ways the outside world is trying to control you. It tries to control your way of thinking and therefore your actions as well. The greatest danger lies in the fact that all this happens without openly informing you, unlike within your family where usually you are told what you should or should not do.

We all live in a system which tries to manipulate us. Imagine yourself as a puppet where someone else is moving your strings without you being aware of it. This system affects all of us, both children and parents. This is why all of us must be equipped with critical thinking in order to protect ourselves against whoever is trying to control our lives not for our own benefit, but for theirs.

C. Who are these powers who try to control us?

P. This will be the focus of my entire conversation with you to follow. Many different agents in the outside world adopt many different ways to influence you in such a way that you will behave like they want you to behave. By doing so, you lose your freedom, you may believe you are taking decisions and forming your opinions on your own, but you're not. I will explain to you who is trying to use you, why they are doing it and how you can protect yourself through critical thinking.

C. You seem to be more concerned than I am.

P. I am indeed concerned because what is at stake is your freedom, the ability to decide for yourself. This is why it's so important to be aware of how many things in the world are structured to have you do what they want. The worst part of it is that they make you believe you're the one who's taking those decisions while you're not. Without critical thinking you'll be like a tool in the hands of someone else, thus losing control of your life. I don't think the idea of being manipulated by someone else is something you would like, would you?

C. Certainly not.

P. Good, so let's dive in and see a number of cases where you can learn how to be independent in your thinking and in your decisions. I will not tell you what you should choose to do in life, I will simply tell you how to protect yourself from anything or anyone attempting to direct you toward certain choices without allowing your own free choice. The world should allow you to form your own ideas and take your own decisions without forcing them upon you. By what I'll describe from here on, you'll see that most often than not, this isn't how the world around you is working.

ED WONNS

A Day at the Soccer Stadium

P. I'll now give you a good example of how people don't make use of critical thinking. It's about the most shocking experience I had in my life when I was your age. It happened when my uncle took me with him to watch a soccer game.

C. The most shocking experience you ever had was watching a soccer game?

P. Yes, it was in Europe. My uncle drove the car to the stadium. On our way, we picked up a guy who was about my uncle's age. For most of the time in the car this guy was silent, he actually appeared to be sad. This struck me, as we were supposed to attend an entertaining event which I imagined had to be something cheerful.

After parking the car close to the stadium and walking toward it, we found ourselves in a huge crowd of people frantically walking and running around us. I had to make sure to keep close to my uncle not to get lost. Everyone was in a frenzy to enter the stadium or to reach the ticket counters on time. My uncle and the other guy sped up, so we were all rushing the same way, like objects carried away in a massive river flow. I felt like a twig carried along by the currents.

C. That sensation was your most shocking experience?

P. Not quite yet, but it was like preparing me to what I would have seen right after. We eventually entered the stadium after climbing up several levels. The stadium from inside looked even bigger than how it appeared from outside. It was a huge container built around the soccer field and hosted over eighty thousand people. All the spectators were flowing onto the concrete grandstands like microscopic dots gradually filling up all the gaps. Every single one of those dots was a person, most of those dots were distant from me, so I couldn't even figure out how each one of those individuals looked like. In the end, shortly before the start of the game, all those dots covered the empty lines of concrete, thus forming a single human tapestry around the field.

When the players entered the field to position themselves for the game, the crowd generated a massive roar. What struck me was the crowd's behavior being totally different versus the players'. People were screaming like hell, some guy around me would direct his screams against this or that other player, while the players were way too far down on the field to be even capable of hearing what the people around me in the crowd were screaming at them.

It was like a one-way communication directed from the crowd to the players. People from the crowd yelled at them, while the players were focusing on their game, regardless of what the crowd was shouting.

C. I still can't see anything so shocking about this.

P. Yet it was, because I was starting to feel a very deep sorrow for those players. I felt extremely sad for them. I noticed with surprise the size of their leg muscles, especially their thighs; they were far greater than how I had seen them on the TV screen at home, where they appeared so skinny. Those strong muscular legs I was seeing live, clearly indicated those players had gone through intense training exercises and great sacrifices in order to become soccer players. Those guys must have worked really hard to become what they were. This was in great contrast with the crowd targeting them with insults.

The man who came with us always kept silent beside me, never saying a word, nervously biting his nails while watching the game. All of a sudden, a goal gets scored, and the entire crowd jumps up generating a devastating boom like as if an atomic bomb had been dropped on us. The concrete row I was sitting on, suddenly started shaking as the result of that boom. At that very moment, the silent man close to me jumped up screaming his head off like as if he'd gone nuts in a split second. I instinctively stood up myself, trying not to disappear under the layer formed by the crowd rising around me.

C. I really don't get what's so shocking. It's basically a soccer game where fans are getting excited over what's going on in the game.

P. This is precisely the point. I was shocked by seeing a massive number of individuals who had lost their individual traits. Instead of being different elements of one group, it was that group, the crowd, which acted as one single element. The individuals were no more so, they were simply anonymous components of a crowd, indistinguishable from one another. I couldn't see this or that guy in the crowd studying or analyzing what was going on in the game. The crowd was driven altogether by basic wild instincts, versus the players who were simply trying to do their job at the best of their skills.

C. But it's all about fans who go to a game and want to see their team winning.

P. Remember what I told you at the start of our conversation about understanding a certain matter as the basis of critical thinking?

C. I sure do, but what has all this to do with it?

P. That's the point: it has absolutely nothing to do with it. All those individuals totally lost their critical thinking by letting themselves get swayed by the crowd. They lost their understanding of the game because all they wanted was to see their team win, or to insult the opposing team. The question you must ask yourself, is why did they so desperately want someone else to win, that is, the players of their favorite team, when they had no part in that team?

The reason is that they were projecting their own wish of winning onto someone else, the players. They yelled insults at the players when these were making mistakes. They displaced their own problems onto the players. The reason they did so, was because they didn't have enough critical thinking to understand this. Critical thinking must also be applied to one's own behavior.

This is true about the guy who was silent in the car with us and was nervously biting his nails when watching the game, but who literally freaked out by jumping off his feet with an uncontrollable scream when a goal was scored on the field.

Was that guy there to really appreciate the skills of the players, or was he there to see his team winning, so he could identify himself in his team and feel happy at that moment just to compensate his failures in his everyday life? Of course, it's the second case scenario. This guy, just like the crowd, was there to discharge the frustrations of his everyday life.

C. Okay, he may not have been happy with his life, so he hoped his favorite soccer team would win to make him somewhat happy. I don't see anything wrong with that.

P. What's wrong is that this guy, just like the crowd he was part of, made no use of critical thinking in order to understand why they were acting the way they were.

C. You really found all this to be so shocking?

P. Yes, absolutely. What was going on that day at the stadium was an example of how single individuals lose their thinking by being part of a crowd driven by pure instincts. This showed me that people are fine about being manipulated by a crowd which takes control of them. I'll show you again later on, how individuals lose control of themselves by being unknowingly turned into a crowd or a group.

C. But, after all, these guys at the stadium wanted to have some excitement. What's wrong with that? Are they guilty of being fans of a soccer team? Should we ban fans from stadiums? If so, you would have no spectators, empty stadiums. Is that what you want?

P. Your questions are justified if you take my considerations to the letter. The reason I described what I saw at the stadium is to pinpoint how fans can become fanatics. How an apparently innocent excitement can degenerate into uncontrolled behavior simply because of no critical thinking. By watching their behavior, I saw how individuals lose their individual thinking and get carried away by the crowd. The group they belong to, ends up controlling them instead of being themselves in control of what they are doing.

There's more to this. I mentioned the guy who was sad and silent for all the time, until he literally exploded into an uncontrolled act of excitement in perfect unison with the mass of people surrounding him. This betrays a concerning psychological condition. This guy appeared to be depressed and compensated his state of depression by identifying himself in the soccer team he supported. He most likely felt miserable, but by identifying himself with his favorite soccer team, he could finally experience success, so his explosive reaction when his team scored the goal, proves that he was desperate to discharge that wish for success which he couldn't experience in his everyday life.

C. Well, in that case it was good for him to have gone to the stadium, so he could have felt happy, and that experience relieved him from his distress.

P. For sure, if you see this as a momentary relief, but the reason why I told you about this guy, is that his behavior pointed to a bigger problem which this guy hadn't thought about enough.

C. How do you know this guy hadn't thought about his problem?

P. It's kind of obvious. He clearly displaced himself onto something else. He generated this sequence of thoughts: I don't win in my life, but I'm like the soccer team I support, the soccer team wins, therefore I'm successful.

Consider his overreaction to the team scoring the goal, it came like an explosion from what appeared to be a depressed state of mind, proving that he wasn't really in control of himself, which betrayed the fact that he hadn't quite understood his own problem. Again: no use of critical thinking.

C. Okay, but you may have been asking too much out of this guy. Maybe he was simply too busy with his own everyday problems, which is why he needed to kill his depression by going to the stadium. Other people in his place may want to go to the disco and dance like crazy.

P. Sure, and, why not, others may want to get drunk or take drugs which kill them. There are different degrees of how badly they will reduce themselves to, but in all cases, they don't understand, or they don't want to understand, the reasons of their condition.

At any rate, by your questions I see you haven't appreciated the extent of my shock when I attended that soccer game. I'm confident that the moment I widen your view from the stadium to the history of mankind, you'll start noticing some similarities between my limited experience at the stadium, versus a broader outlook on society and history.

C. You're telling me that what's going on in a soccer stadium is similar to what we read in history books?

P. Yes, absolutely. The very reason of my shock is that, unlike in a history book where you read about events which you can only imagine, at the stadium I found myself right there within, directly confronted with the event. Up to that moment, I had watched soccer games only on TV, which conveyed none of those sensations about the crowd, which I was having right there inside the stadium.

It's like reading a book about a heretic preacher who lived hundreds of years ago, being burned alive in front of a large crowd because of his ideas against the Catholic Church. You may well be reading about that event in a lazy and undistressed way, like when you have some history class homework. Reading about it will never give you the sensations of actually finding yourself right there in the crowd, watching and cheering the burning to death of a human being.

C. Isn't it far-fetched to assimilate a soccer game to the execution of a person?

P. Not at all, because of those similarities I pointed to. You have to consider that in both cases you see individuals losing their individuality in favor of being parts of one group. In that crowd-packed stadium, each one of those tiny dots was actually a human being, but there was nothing human about that scene, all you could perceive was the presence of a single uniform mass. I felt scared at the idea I was part of that mass.

I related that scene to what I was reading on history books, about conflicts and devastations caused by large groups of people. The aggressive, instinctual and not thoughtful attitude of the crowd in that stadium made me think: by seeing what I see here, I now understand how millions of people caused catastrophes in human history.

C. You mean to say that if humans were more thoughtful and less instinctive, the making of history would be better?

P. I see you're getting closer to the idea. I'll address later on again how your obedience to a group can destroy your critical thinking. Right now, I want to move on and consider your immediate surroundings: how you should deal with the people you find around yourself.

ED WONNS

The People Around You

P. I want to talk to you about how you should deal with the people around you, and what you should be watchful about. Remember the subject of our conversation, it's critical thinking. One thing to be aware of, is whether the people around you use critical thinking. For our purpose, we'll call idiots all those people who make little or no use of critical thinking. However, you may have a different idea of someone we define as an idiot. How would you define an idiot?

C. I'd say a person with low intelligence.

P. That is very true as a general definition of what an idiot is. However, I want to narrow down the concept when addressing critical thinking. Strictly speaking, a person who doesn't make much use of critical thinking may very well not be considered an idiot by common standards. As an example, there may be someone who is proficient in some activity which requires a significant amount of intelligence, yet for our standards we may still consider that person to be an idiot.

C. I don't get it. You have someone proving she's intelligent and you would consider her an idiot all the same?

P. Yes, when that person lacks the understanding of being manipulated by others and repeats ideas taken from others, without having carefully thought over those ideas.

I'll give you an example: say we have an engineer who's very clever in designing certain machinery and, by doing so, proves to be intelligent and certainly not an idiot according to common standards. However, the moment you question that engineer over her vision of the world and facts of life, you may notice her ideas are articulated in a way which betrays they haven't been thought over, but simply taken as good from some other source.

Even if that person proves to be intelligent to a certain extent, that same person may very well be manipulated and controlled by others, since she doesn't use her intelligence to prevent such control of her mind. Therefore, that intelligent person may very well be an idiot for our own present standards and can add up with others to form a population of useful idiots, that is, people who are unaware of being used by other people whose interests are different from their own.

C. You're displaying a scenario where part of the population is using and controlling another part of the population made up of what you define here as idiots. This doesn't seem to be a fair society. How can we prevent this state of things?

P. I will get to that toward the end of this part of our conversation.

Before getting to it, I want to draw a distinction over essentially two different types of idiots.

The first type is what we already described, it's about a person who's intelligent but doesn't use that intelligence to think critically.

The second type is a person who has very low intelligence. It's the typical definition you mentioned earlier.

One would assume that we have some hope with idiots of the first type because they have intelligence, and little or no hope with idiots of the second type because they lack intelligence, which is always at the basis of critical thinking.

C. I would assume people with mental impairment or deficiency are part of the second group, for example people who were born with some brain malfunction.

P. This may be the case, but may also be not. We should never, ever, believe that someone with a clear mental deficiency, for example someone who cannot put a sentence together, is that second type of idiot we describe. If we were to jump to conclusions marking someone as an idiot just because, for example, someone else has determined to confine that person to a structure for the mentally ill, without us having any additional information other than that, we wouldn't be using critical thinking ourselves, so we would be the real idiots, not the person who is being treated for mental illness!

C. But if we realize a person can't put together anything which makes any sense, and we still refuse to consider that person an idiot, we would be denying evidence.

P. Not necessarily. Sometimes we notice something which appears to be evident, but it may not tell us the truth. Here's where an idea from a philosopher of the seventeenth century, by the name of Descartes, helps me to explain my point.

Descartes' concern was to define something he could consider true. What can we hold as being true? Things appear to be true, but what we believe is their real being may not be what they are, rather what they appear to be. Therefore, all things considered, what is really true? I may be led to think nothing is true, because I can always doubt something is true.

However, at one point, Descartes had this thought: "Hey, wait a minute! I see what is really true: it's my doubting! I'm totally sure that I'm doubting. That's one thing I'm sure about, so it's true."

He goes on to say that since he's sure he's doubting, then he's thinking, so if he's thinking, this means he exists and therefore cannot doubt his own existence.

C. All this sounds very logical, but I don't see where you're trying to bring me.

P. I'm trying to bring you toward the idea that doubting is the very foundation of critical thinking. This argument by Descartes is a perfect example of critical thinking because it starts from doubting and, from there, reaches a conclusion. I start doubting, and from there I know I exist.

We were talking about whom we should consider an idiot. Just because some people may think someone is an idiot, we must not take that idea for granted. We must doubt what anyone else says, and we must start drawing our own conclusions, only after having considered all possible explanations of a certain condition.

This example taken from the philosopher tells us exactly what critical thinking is: it's a method. This means it's a way of thinking which gives us a deeper insight into things.

What matters in first place isn't the conclusion we will reach over something, but how we reach that conclusion. Casting doubts allows us to overcome them by asking ourselves if those same doubts make sense and, from there, reach a better understanding of things.

This will protect us from ideas which other people will try to force on us, because we will dissect those ideas and see if they are wrongful or not, before accepting them as good.

C. Very well, you gave me a lot of abstract ideas, but how do I practically figure out who's an idiot in the sense you describe?

P. There are various cases.

First off, since we just touched upon the essential role of doubt in critical thinking, a real idiot has very few doubts. A real idiot has more certainty than doubts, if you recall what I just said about the essential role of doubt in critical thinking.

Along these lines, another philosopher, Socrates, used to say: "I know that I know nothing". This doesn't imply you must doubt everything at all times in order to be sure you're not an idiot. Doubts are part of the process which helps you find the truth in things.

Now I need to get back to your question addressing some practical examples. More often than not, an idiot has a high opinion of herself. However, also people who make great use of critical thinking may just as well have a high opinion of themselves. The difference lies in the way the idiot and the critical thinker acquire a high opinion of themselves.

An idiot feels intelligent, smart, clever and whatever other great intellective qualities you may think of, because the idiot takes it as a matter of fact. This great opinion of oneself is not the result of self-criticism, it's simply a given matter of fact.

On the other hand, the critical thinker reaches a high opinion of herself by acknowledging she went through doubts and self-criticism.

In short: a significant clue which betrays an idiot is lack of self-criticism. That is something you want to stay on the watch for.

C. What other clues may lead me to identify an idiot?

P. Listen to other people's opinions and ideas. Try to figure out if what they say is the result of their own thinking, or whether they simply copy/paste ideas from others into their own mind.

One way to understand if this is the case, is to ask them to explain the reasons of their thoughts. The moment they provide an articulate reply which follows a logical sequence, you know they haven't simply heard something and have stuck to it.

In case their explanations of their opinions are too short and basic, that's usually a sign they are taking thoughts from others and are keeping them as good without actually having pondered over them.

C. How about if they bluntly learn the entire sequence of thoughts from someone else and say it to me? I may be led to believe they have elaborated their ideas by themselves.

P. This is apparently true. They may very well learn a series of ideas as well as the arguments proving those ideas, without any use of critical thinking. However, if you listen carefully to what they say, you may spot contradictions in their reasoning, which prove their ideas aren't coherent. Should you have the impression they are just repeating ideas they picked up from others, you can challenge them and see if there's any lack of logic between their ideas.

When ideas are simply learned by heart rather than being the result of thoughtful reasoning, you will notice they are just kept together as adjacent parts, but not as parts of a logical chain.

C. Can you give me an example of what you mean by this?

P. One trick you can adopt, is to ask very general questions. Replies to general questions are far more challenging because they imply a certain amount of information to be analyzed. Instead, if you ask a specific question, there will be less information to work on.

An example of a general question is: do you believe God exists? It sounds like a specific question, but it's a general question in its essence because it concerns our own existence.

Instead, an example of a specific question is: how many hours per day should you allocate to your homework? This second question can be addressed by knowing one's own load of homework and schedule, it doesn't require much critical thinking.

As to the first question about the existence of God, the type of reply you get sheds light over the amount of critical thinking involved.

On the lower end, the reply could be something like: "God exists because my parents told me so, and I believe them". This reply clearly displays itself as a copy/paste type of idea. I hear the idea and I make it mine without thinking it over.

On the higher end, the reply could be something like: "That's what we are told by many religions, and it may explain why we exist. We are limited as humans, so we should consider the existence of a supernatural entity which explains our existence. We refer to that entity as God".

The more you challenge others, the more you can understand by their replies if they reflect our definition of idiots.

Quite obviously, when evaluating what people around you are saying, you must rely on your own critical thinking. When you ask a general question, your first concern has to be on how the question is answered by the other person, not if the answer provides the solution.

C. You're telling me the way they answer is more important than the content of the answer?

P. Let me clarify: what matters in first place is to set a problem and see how it gets addressed and elaborated, regardless whether a solution to the problem is found. Sometimes a definitive solution to a number of problems will never be found. If we knew all solutions to all problems we would be God.

What I mean is that the articulate reply to the question about the existence of God leads you to understand how the person who gives you that reply sets the terms of the problem, even if the solution still remains open to debate.

In our example, the solution is "we should consider the existence of a supernatural entity" starting from the problem that "we are limited as humans".

The important part of this reasoning is the acknowledgement of our human limitations which emphasizes the problem, as we realize in first place that we aren't God. This by itself implies a certain thinking depth.

C. Problems are more important than solutions?

P. In a nutshell: think in terms of problems first, then seek solutions. Try to reach a solution when possible, but never put the solution in front of the problem, which is the case of the example of the basic reply saying "God exists because I was told so". In such a statement, the solution overrides the problem. The person making that statement proves she hasn't set the problem, and took the solution for granted.

C. Therefore, critical thinking implies setting problems before solutions and reaching solutions, if possible, after having set the problems in a clear way. It's all about asking yourself questions in first place.

P. It is definitely so, because reality is complex. We must not be afraid to collect problems one after the other, and we must avoid jumping straight to conclusions without having first worked on the problems, otherwise any conclusion or solution will be meaningless.

We also have to consider how you have to ask yourself questions when addressing any matter. It's essential to ask yourself those questions and identify problems keeping your mindset void of any preferred solution or bias. If you are biased on a certain matter, which means you already have certain ideas and opinions on what you are trying to understand, that's a huge obstacle to any proper understanding, and therefore, to critical thinking.

C. Can you provide an example on how bias can be an obstacle to my understanding of things?

P. Loads of examples to pick. Suffice to pick this one. Say you like a certain group of friends, and one day they are reported as authors of some criminal action. Instead of not believing the news by thinking they would never have done that, simply because they're your friends, you should actually check the facts at the best of your knowledge without considering they're friends of yours. In other words, without any bias taking over your investigation of the event.

As a conclusion of our description of those we defined as idiots for the purpose of our conversation which is focused on critical thinking, idiots will be easily manipulated by others who will make them think and act how they want.

One more example is a military environment. When you are a soldier of the army, strictly speaking, you must be an idiot, as you mustn't raise doubts or questions, but simply execute orders.

C. How about if idiots like to be manipulated, how about if they like to find themselves in that condition? Maybe they're happier than others who aren't idiots?

P. That's possible at first sight, however their condition leaves them unaware of being manipulated. Their temporary state of happiness may easily turn into sadness and depression, the moment they realize they aren't the real authors of their decisions.

If they understood how and why they were manipulated, they wouldn't be idiots anymore, and they could aspire to having their condition changed.

C. Perhaps many people don't ask themselves that many questions, they simply want to get on with their life, and it's okay for them.

P. This is the mindset we need to fight against, for our own well-being and dignity. Later on in our conversation, I'll show you many cases where you will see how important it is to retain your own freedom through critical thinking and be the boss of yourself. I'm sure you'll start seeing all the advantages of being able to take control of your own life rather than having others do it for you. Freedom and critical thinking go hand in hand.

C. It'll be interesting if, by adopting your suggestions, I'll detect any idiots around me.

P. Sure, but identifying idiots isn't enough. You may have around people you consider friends who aren't idiots in the sense we described, but who can still involve you in a toxic friendship.

C. Toxic friendship?

P. Yes, it happens when one or more friends around you have a negative influence on you, a toxic one, like poison. They behave in a way which makes you think and act against what is good for you. Your critical thinking is necessary to understand you have to detach yourself from such so-called friends.

Let's take a simple example. You may find yourself meeting people who take drugs, drink alcoholic beverages or smoke. You may think you like those people and trust them, deciding to follow their suggestions. By doing so you can go down a path where you will lose control of yourself.

C. On another note, can idiots turn into their opposite, like become critical thinkers?

P. Yes, definitely. We don't call them idiots because of a persistent lack of intelligence, as the general notion suggests. We proved how intelligent people can be in fact idiots by simply making little or no use of critical thinking. The reverse may apply to people regarded as dumb or stupid. You may be surprised to learn that people addressed as idiots according to the general notion, may be hiding surprising mental capabilities.

C. What can we do to prevent people from acting like idiots?

P. We should share the content of our present conversation with the greatest possible number of people. We want to trigger everyone's hidden desire to think in a free and independent manner, we want to overcome laziness. See, quite often we leave aside critical thinking because it requires effort, but we want people to understand they will be rewarded by raising doubts and questions which will give them a better understanding of the world around them and freedom from being manipulated by others.

ED WONNS

Your School Teacher

P. I want to start off from where we left, about how we can help others make use of critical thinking, when they listen to our present conversation.

This can also happen at school when you interact with your classmates. However, your interaction with your teacher is different, versus the one with your classmates. This is because at school you usually receive far more information from your teacher, versus the information you give to your teacher. You have to listen more to the teacher, versus the teacher having to listen to you. It's more of a one-way communication from the teacher to you, rather than a two-way exchange of information like you would typically have with your classmates. You are the one who's supposed to learn at school. The typical school setting doesn't consider the scenario where the teacher learns from you.

There are several things to be aware of about teachers. We'll start off from there, to see how you can make use of critical thinking in your relationship with your teacher.

C. You're telling me I should filter everything the teacher tells me, by using the method you described? Like the philosopher you mentioned, Descartes, I should be doubting about all the information the teacher gives me and consider it as true only after having it carefully analyzed and verified?

P. That is so. You must use your critical thinking on any source of information, call it a teacher, a friend, a parent, the news, the internet and so on.

C. But if that'll be the case, I may start getting into arguments with teachers, by doubting or criticizing what they say.

P. Not necessarily. First off, a good teacher will welcome any remarks from you which may allow her to explain her point better. You also have to consider that you must first ponder over any doubt or criticism. As we saw, critical thinking doesn't mean you have to criticize whatever you come across. You rather have to review the information you receive, think it over at your best and, only after doing so, come out with a reasonable argument.

C. How do I know I have a good teacher?

P. Great question, I was getting to it. This may sound disappointing, but there aren't that many really good teachers. It's like considering different professions in everyday life. For example, not all doctors are as good as they should be, same for lawyers or any other profession.

Speaking of teachers up to high school included, there's hardly a chance you'll be able to choose the teacher you want. She will be assigned to you just like your parents. Parents set in with you as a child, and you have to take the parents you get. On the other hand, you can choose your friends. By the way, this doesn't imply your friends are better than your parents just because you can choose them. They have different roles, and we assume parents care for you the most, but we don't want to get carried away now by comparing teachers, parents, and friends.

The point I'm making, is that you'll have to live with the teacher who's assigned to you.

C. I have to be lucky enough to come across the right teacher.

P. That is definitely so. However, by what I'll tell you shortly, you'll see that you may help your teacher improve. By highlighting some unclear areas or contradictions in what the teacher says, you may force her to reconsider her own teaching in a positive way.

C. This means I could get the teacher more into critical thinking?

P. For sure, when you ask questions on some aspects which the teacher hasn't fully covered. This will force the teacher to review and maybe even change her previous explanations.

Now, let me tell you a few things to be aware of about teachers. As a general notion, not all people who understand matters perfectly, can explain those matters just as well to others. Teaching is an art by itself. You may find people who have a deep understanding of something, but who may not be successful in conveying that understanding to others.

Back again to what you rightly said, you must be lucky to come across the right teacher because in that case you'll realize the teacher will address matters through critical thinking before you even start doing the same.

C. How can I understand when a teacher is making use of critical thinking?

P. If you remember what we said so far about critical thinking, you'll see clues of it in the adopted teaching method. Rather than giving you a bunch of information to learn, the teacher will question that same information. As we said earlier, critical thinking implies a problematic approach, identifying problems rather than solely reporting facts.

C. Can you give me some examples?

P. Sure, let's take your history teacher who will tell you about the discovery of America.

When her teaching isn't enlightened by critical thinking, the teacher may tell you how Christopher Columbus sailed across the Atlantic Ocean in 1492 and ran into land unknown up to that moment, which he thought were the Indies he had reached by sailing westbound rather than eastbound. The teacher will go on to say that after his trip, more of the same kind followed, initiating a colonization process of North and South America and so on.

This description tells facts, but doesn't address them in a critical way.

Addressing the same event in a critical way, implies questions to be answered, therefore problems to be considered. One question could be: why do we always mention Columbus as the person who discovered the continent later named America, when five centuries before him the Vikings from Northern Europe had landed on that same continent? The latter is proven by archeological findings, yet the discovery of that continent by the Vikings is barely considered in history books.

Another question is: why did it take so long for Europeans to sail across the Atlantic Ocean and stumble upon that huge continent so late in time, considering they had those sailing capabilities even centuries before?

This last question is about understanding why that discovery took place at that point in history. Once you dig deeper and deeper into those reasons, you'll find out that Columbus is just the tip of the iceberg. Below the tip are important social, economic, cultural developments which explain why time was ripe for someone to sail far out into the Atlantic Ocean at that very moment in history.

As you may have noticed, I just barely started providing a simple example of good teaching, and my reply to your question is getting way longer than what it usually is. This shows you how much more effort is required by addressing an event in history with critical thinking, versus reporting the facts. The moment we try to find an answer to those few questions I highlighted about Columbus' discovery of America, a book hundreds of pages long may not be enough to include all those answers.

The history teacher who explains events without applying critical thinking is mentally lazy. Critical thinking requires effort and persistence, always.

C. You made me curious about some questions you raised. You posed the question about why the discovery by the Vikings is neglected, even if they stepped on North American soil five centuries before Columbus. Why is it so?

P. Setting aside other migration events which occurred thousands of years before the Vikings and Columbus, when populations moved eastbound from the Pacific Ocean and reached what we call today North and South America, the reason why Columbus' trip in 1492 is considered to represent the discovery of America, even if it actually wasn't, has to do with the historical relevance of that action.

Many events may technically be very similar to each other, but one of them becomes history because of its influence over what happens after it takes place. The discovery by the Vikings hasn't brought a wide impact on world history, to our knowledge so far.

I'll give you a different example: many people get shot and killed in this country every year, but if one of those people is the President of the country, you bet it will be reported in history books, unlike the others who will fill criminal statistics in most cases.

C. Makes sense. How about the other question you raised, but didn't quite answer, over why it took so long for Europeans to discover America, considering they had the sailing capabilities to do so, centuries before Columbus?

P. I won't get too deep into the matter now, as I don't want us to get distracted from the focus of our conversation. I'll give you a short answer. Any important historical event is the result of multiple factors which give rise to that event.

Just to take one more example of a bad history teacher, we can consider the start of World War I. A bad teacher will tell you how Archduke Franz Ferdinand was killed in the city of Sarajevo in 1914 and, as a result of that event, various European countries started war at each other.

This is clearly a superficial explanation of events. Many political, social, national and economic factors were brewing in the background of that event. That event was simply the moment which allowed all those other far more important underlying factors to reveal themselves as being the effective reasons which actually generated World War I.

The same holds true for Columbus' trip. Even if sufficient sailing capabilities were available centuries before Columbus, the political, economic, social, cultural preconditions which allowed Columbus' trip hadn't yet developed to that point. Were Columbus never born, someone else in his place would have very likely sailed west like he did, at the same time he lived. This is proven by several trips of other navigators who started long exploratory journeys just a few years before Columbus.

Short and easy answers explaining the reasons of historical events are similar to the short and easy explanations of events in ordinary life. They are shortcuts which prevent you from understanding the real meaning of events.

C. Therefore, setting new questions which require new answers may also allow you to better understand events.

P. Not only, it may pave the way to new discoveries. All great discoveries of mankind are based on critical thinking. Progress in any intellective activity is often marked by huge leaps forward initiated by single individuals who overcame the general thinking, by coming up with ideas which appeared unacceptable to most people of their time. Nevertheless, through effort and persistence they succeeded in opening new avenues for mankind. In order to be effective, the critical thinking mindset must also go along with effort and persistence.

C. A teacher having this mindset could mould her students into a class of free and successful critical thinkers.

P. Yes, absolutely. Students who acquire the thinking method we described, will always set questions trying to find answers to those questions.

C. If that's the teacher's mindset, then she should welcome questions from her students.

P. Yes, because those questions may allow the teacher to see her teaching subject in a new light. A good teacher must establish a two-way communication flow. If the premise is to have an active agent, the teacher, and a passive agent, the student, where information flows in one direction only, this means the teacher has all the knowledge, while students are simple containers to be filled with that knowledge. This scenario is typical of a bad teacher.

C. Therefore, the teacher should allow her students to raise problems.

P. It is precisely so, because this entails that two-way communication flow which triggers more questions, more possible solutions, and ultimately, a better understanding of the subject.

C. However, this may be truer for some subjects, for example history, versus other subjects, for example math, which leaves less room for discussion.

P. Not at all. Critical thinking must be applied across the board. A good math teacher will explain to you how, contrary to the common notion, math can be an opinion.

C. How's that possible?

P. Thanks to scientists and mathematicians who exercised critical thinking, so-called exact sciences have been found not to be quite as exact as they claim to be.

Geometry can be taken as an example of this. For over two thousand years, Euclidean geometry was considered the only possible geometry, until a couple of centuries ago several mathematicians proved the validity of other geometries not based on the principles set by Euclid. A good math teacher should make her students aware of such differences and developments within an exact science.

ED WONNS

The News

P.We talked about how the flow of communication between teacher and students is mostly unidirectional, meaning that information flows from the teacher to the students, rather than being bidirectional, flowing both ways, even if a bidirectional flow is always positive, as it allows the teacher to work on feedback from her students, improving the quality of her own teaching.

Reading or listening to the news is a unidirectional flow, as information is broadcast to millions, if not billions, of people as passive recipients. In recent times, with the advent of the internet this process has changed, since users interact with sources of news through their own devices such as smartphones or computers. This becomes a bidirectional flow, and we'll soon dedicate time to its analysis.

What we consider right now is the unidirectional flow of news, when we're passive recipients of information from the media, when we don't interact with it like we would through our devices connected to the internet. I'm talking about news on TV channels or on the radio, newspapers, magazines, advertisements, etc.

We want to ask ourselves how we should deal with this mass of information which gets thrown at us.

C. I bet you'll tell me we have to analyze it by using critical thinking.

P. You guessed it! Sorry for not providing some alternate starting point, but this is what our conversation is all about.

When it comes to information you receive from the media, I'm sorry to say you'll need a lot, I repeat, a lot of critical thinking, because the outlook on this matter is pretty grim.

The first thing you need to consider is the source of the information you receive. Each time you watch, read or listen to the news, you must be aware of who's behind the source of the news.

Say you watch a certain news channel on TV, it's important to know as much as possible about who owns and operates that channel before following the news it broadcasts. With the exception of very few sources of information structured to deliver contents which are generated through critical thinking, the vast majority of information sources worldwide are structured to deliver information crafted by the political or economic interests of the owners of those same sources.

C. You're telling me that most news channels are tools of propaganda?

P. Yes, most definitely. The more you develop your own skills in filtering whatever is fed to you, the more you realize how the news is structured not to inform you, but to manipulate you.

As we explained earlier, you must have a method. A few basic steps have to be followed. The first rule of this method is to cast doubts on whatever information is given to you. This must be your approach. It's not a negative approach implying that all you're fed is fake news, it's a suspension of judgement. You have to suspend your approval before considering something true, until you carry out its verification.

As I mentioned, in first place ask yourself who is behind the source of the news. As an example, if a certain TV channel is sponsored by people affiliated to a certain political party, you can bet that news will be manipulated according to the interests of that political party.

Bearing this in mind, you have to ask yourself what is the ultimate source the news is taken from. You know your immediate source is that specific TV channel, but the next question is where did that channel get that news from?

Since in most cases you cannot witness events directly in person, you must try to compare as many possible sources of news you can, in order to establish similarities and differences between the same subject matter broadcast by different sources.

This last step is crucial because it's extremely helpful in selecting along the way some specific source of news which is more truthful than others. It goes without saying that most times these more reliable sources are generated by free-thinking individuals who aren't controlled by powers of sorts, hence they genuinely seek a deep understanding of events. More often than not, academics who dedicate their lives to studying events of the world, are more trusted than journalists who typically reflect the political or economic stance of the media they work for.

C. Therefore, I should privilege information from academics rather than journalists?

P. No, not necessarily. What matters is a thoughtful analysis of the information itself. Thereafter, it's crucial to be aware of the source of that information. At times, you may find some journalists are more trustworthy than academics.

To make things worse, even highly ranked academics who are detached from any specific power and dedicate their lives to studying, often find themselves disagreeing with others in their own group, over the interpretation of facts and events.

C. How can I make my way through all this mass of news when even highly educated professors can have very different ideas on the same events?

P. I'll start off with some practical examples. If we take an event like a bank robbery, our comparative analysis between what gets reported by different sources may not yield much insight, as the only ultimate source of information may be a statement from the police, which is the same starting point of the news given by different outlets. Therefore, for this purpose, let's take a more complex event such as a war going on between two different countries.

You may find out that historians who have dedicated their lives to studying the events in those countries may have considerably different opinions. They may have accessed all possible sources of information analyzing them in depth, basically applying our critical thinking method. However, they may still find themselves at odds in the conclusions of their respective studies. One historian may see the war as a result of economic developments, another may instead see it as a result of political developments. We may assume both historians apply our approach based on critical thinking and yet reach different conclusions.

C. This may prove that critical thinking brings you nowhere in terms of understanding events.

P. Critical thinking isn't a magic wand which guarantees definitive solutions to problems or undisputable interpretations of what is studied. It rather works like a filter. When you let one hundred individuals provide their one hundred different interpretations of a certain complex event, those individuals who adopted our method based on critical thinking, will have ruled out basic nonsense. It's like as if you have all these different interpretations of the same events pass through a filter. Those which haven't been critically analyzed will pass through the filter as nonsense. The filter will retain all other interpretations which were guided by critical thinking.

The interpretations not discarded by our filter may still bear differences between them, however they will not contain nonsensical or superficial arguments. Even if the ultimate truth may not be ascertained, we can establish different degrees of truthfulness.

C. Therefore, establishing the truth about certain events may still have a long way to go, even through the filter of critical thinking.

P. Not reaching the ultimate truth doesn't imply there aren't different degrees of truthfulness. There may always be a long way to go, but you have to consider how often you come across people who throw out theories about events without even knowing the facts themselves. Analyzing events and the news of those events requires a lot of effort. It entails collecting information and hard evidence about those events. The moment your interpretation is retained by our filter which discards other nonsensical interpretations, it will be easy for you to debunk everything which wasn't processed through critical thinking, and you'll have the upper hand in proving your point against others.

Keep in mind that any news will never describe facts and events in a perfectly objective way, aside from extremely short statements like communicating, for example, the arrival of the president of one country visiting another country, such as the statement: "The plane of the President of the U.S. landed in Canada today at 2:00 PM".

The moment this event is expanded into describing the reasons of that visit and the reactions of people to that visit, news of that same event from different sources will differ, as they will be generated by selecting and prioritizing different elements. This means that the news contains interpretation whether we like it or not, because it necessarily follows a selective process when putting facts together.

However, when applying your own critical thinking filter to all possible news, facts and events, you reach a degree of truthfulness which is always greater than what comes from other people who don't apply that filter.

Even if two very well-educated historians may have different opinions on certain events, their opinions will still be worth a lot more than the opinions of people who didn't embark on the tough journey of analyzing facts and events with critical thinking.

Simply consider how many people throw out theories of events without having any knowledge of those events.

How often do you hear clear-cut opinions about events in the world from people who haven't taken the time to study or even learn those events? The grim answer to the question is: very often and more often than you would believe.

Any discussion between individuals will always be more fruitful the moment those individuals have taken the time to learn what they're talking about. We said it quite a few times by now: it takes effort to acquire information, to learn it and to understand it. It's easier to follow a certain interpretation or theory of events, without even learning the facts, simply because it may sound to go along well with your own biases, interests, or even laziness.

Critical Thinking and Values

P. After having provided a number of examples of critical thinking, we have to consider its relationship to values.

C. What do you mean by values?

P. Values define what is important for an individual. Values are closely related to morals, meaning that morals are values upheld by people as a group. Values are decisive in shaping one's actions.

We defined critical thinking as a value itself because it allows us not to be manipulated by others. We therefore retain our own freedom of judgement and, ultimately, freedom of action.

By taking a closer look at this relationship, you see that our freedom of thought and action are the real values underlying critical thinking. The latter is basically a tool aimed at realizing those values. Our main concern behind developing critical thinking is to be intellectively free and in control of ourselves.

C. How can you argue this individual idea of being in control of your own thoughts and actions should also be a collective principle, good for all?

P. It follows necessarily. Any group of people is a sum of individuals. By saying we want each individual to think with her own head, any group will be the result of more individuals thinking with their own head.

C. If that's the case, it will be very difficult for groups to form morals, as individuals in a group are supposed to give up their own views in favor of those of the group they belong to.

P. The validity of common values will always be targeted by critical thinking. However, critical thinking can break up collective ideas and result in new collective ideas, as we have seen in history.

C. Such as?

P. I'll take an example of a great critical thinker who brought about a revolution in the history of Christianity. Christianity was a revolutionary historical change itself through one individual, Jesus Christ. However, for the purpose of my example, I will narrow it down to a reformer whose thoughts and actions provide a direct idea of what I mean. I'm talking about Martin Luther, a Christian monk who was born in 1483 in Eisleben, a small town which is now part of Germany. This was nine years before the discovery of the American continent by

Christopher Columbus whom we took as an example when we talked about teaching at school.

Martin Luther studied and followed the preaching of the Bible. By using his critical thinking, he realized that the Catholic Church of his time, who placed herself as an intermediary structure between man and God, was essentially a structure of power aimed at manipulating its constituents with the purpose of serving its own interests in place of God. A famous case was the sale of indulgences. By paying a certain amount of money to the Catholic Church, one would have her own sins forgiven. Luther sharply uncovered the lies imposed by this system and started a general movement aimed at restoring God's role, as opposed to the Catholic Church who established herself as a necessary intermediary in order to interact with God.

One single man, Luther, by exercising his critical thinking, destroyed the building of lies held by the Catholic Church to preserve her power over the people of his time.

C. Therefore, Martin Luther set the beginning of a new era just like Columbus when he sailed out across the ocean. However, you had explained that Columbus had success because the conditions of his time allowed him to realize his idea. The same should hold true for Luther as well.

P. Yes, absolutely. I'm happy to see you understood my point about Columbus, and it certainly applies to Luther's case just as it does to any other historical event.

Had Luther lived, say, a hundred years before his time, he would have likely been executed by arson by the Catholic Church, as was the fate of another religious reformer, Jan Hus, who had attempted to change things before him. However, Luther lived at a time when new social and political conditions had developed to a point allowing for his protection from being executed, while his free thinking spread itself to many others of his time.

C. Why did you pick this example of Luther after the one of Columbus?

P. I took the example of Columbus to show how history should be taught. I take the example of Luther to show how critical thinking can spread from one individual to others, up to forming a large group of people having values in common. In other words, to show how some well-founded ideas proving a wrong state of things can improve that same state of things.

C. Critical thinking always produces positive changes?

P. Yes, when applied by individuals who are victims of an external force trying to coerce them into following its will by reducing or killing their freedom.

C. What do you exactly mean here?

P. I mean that someone may have enough critical thinking to be aware that a certain system is designed to subdue people, but will decide to keep that system in place for the sake of her own interests.

I'll soon explain what I mean by this, when talking about your smartphone and social media.

The point is that critical thinking must be thought of as a tool for a person to free herself from any type of domination. By doing so, it reaches its socially useful target. It's an individual value turning into a social value. Since thought inspires and guides action, freedom of thinking is freedom of action.

Your Phone

P. We addressed various environments where you need to rely on critical thinking in order to maintain your freedom of thought and action, that is, when dealing with the people around you, your school teacher, and the news. By explaining how you should cope with all these different situations, I believe we have set a solid foundation for the use of critical thinking, so now time is ripe to move on and consider the clear and present dangers of our technocratic society.

C. What do you mean by technocratic society?

P. Today, more than ever in history, technology plays a major role in society. Technology is used by a tiny part of the world's population to control the remaining vast majority. You find evidence of this in the very intrusive use of technology. Governments take advantage of the unprecedented availability of technological means, and a very small number of people within state-owned entities or corporations control the inner workings of smartphones and social media, which are two main avenues where the intrusive control of the population takes place. We'll first consider how this happens with smartphones, thereafter we'll focus on social media.

I want to give you some historical perspective on what is arguably the most important technological device we carry with us today: the smartphone. By smartphone, I mean a mobile handheld phone with computer-like functions, a touchscreen, and capable of browsing the web. I can never stress enough the significance of the revolution brought about by the internet and smartphones together.

C. What kind of revolution?

P. A revolution in the way we access information and behave in relation to it. For the first time in the history of mankind we see a radical change which occurred in the last three decades, though most of this change occurred in the last fifteen years.

If you draw a straight horizontal line on a very long wall and put a sign marking one thousand years for every yard of the line, you'll need a wall which is at least three hundred yards long to include the history of mankind. The end of this line is where we stand today.

Right there within the last yard you can mark a portion equal to our last three decades. Its length on the line will be a little over one inch, compared to the yard reflecting the last one thousand years.

C. If I get the proportion right, you're telling me that if you take the last inch of the line and compare it to the previous three hundred yards, it's like taking the last thirty years or so, and comparing them to the history of mankind.

P. Yes, though keep in mind we can't really set an exact date for the evolutionary change from ape to man. The earliest ancestors of the human species are dated back to six million years ago. We're considering the start of mankind when our current species, homo sapiens, made its first appearance on earth, around three hundred thousand years ago.

The most radical change ever on how information is spread across the globe, happened and is still happening within that single inch of linear time we currently find ourselves in, versus the three hundred yards preceding it.

I'm actually being generous by giving this change a time frame of three decades because it's even shorter, considering the greatest spread of smartphones worldwide occurred in the last decade alone. One billion users were registered in 2012, while today that number is almost five times as much.

C. What happened in the last three decades?

P. In the nineties we had the first rudimental smartphones, in 2007 the first iPhone by Apple, in 2009 the first smartphone by Samsung. Today in 2025, smartphone users are almost sixty percent of the world population which is over eight billion people.

C. How about the internet?

P. Likewise, the origins of the World Wide Web which gave rise to the internet, date back to the nineties thanks in great part to the work of computer scientist Tim Berners-Lee who invented protocols which expanded internet usage to the general public. From there on, internet access increased in a similar way to the growing use of smartphones.

C. You're telling me about this revolution happening in the most recent tiny bit of history we're at now, but how about other revolutions brought about by the invention of the telephone, the car, the airplane? They all took place less than one hundred and fifty years ago and changed our lives as well.

P. They sure did, but all those technological revolutions didn't expand across the world population by any means as fast as the current revolution, without considering a new one which just started brought by artificial intelligence.

C. Why is it so important for you to highlight the speed at which the internet and smartphones have changed the world?

P. Every technological revolution brings along a surprise effect which is associated with a sense of marvel. It's a shock, and like every shock, we can adapt and recover from it when we're given enough time to assess its nature. After the first phones, cars and planes were invented, the world population had many decades to adapt to these new means of communication and transport, as it took a far more significant amount of time for these means to be employed on an effective global scale, versus the revolution we're considering at the moment.

Taking the 2007 launch of the first iPhone as our milestone, in less than two decades most of the people in the world have found themselves with the largest ever amount of information available in their pockets.

C. Okay, but I'm still failing to understand why a time frame of a few less decades for the diffusion of smartphones versus, say, cars, is so important for what you call a revolution to take place.

P. I see something much deeper about the nature of this revolution. The greater speed at which it's taking place raises my concerns about understanding the negative effects pertaining to its unique nature and coping with them in due time.

All things considered, traditional phones, cars and planes made it easier for us to communicate and move around, but I don't deem their impact on people's brains as meaningful as having billions of people constantly receiving information from a device positioned a few inches from their face often for several hours in a day. It's a totally new interface between the individual and the world, whose presence raises very serious questions.

C. What questions?

P. In first place, can we fully assess the significance of a revolution at the time we're living it? We're living through a momentous historical event which we may call the rise of the internet and smartphones combined. Just like any major event in history, we have a better understanding of it a long time after it happens.

C. I'm struggling to follow you on this.

P. I'll take you back to my example of the discovery of the American continent. The Vikings set their foot on North American soil several centuries before Christopher Columbus. The moment they landed on today's Eastern coast of Canada, they may well have believed their discovery was the dawning of a new era. However, it wasn't so, as the impact on world history of the discovery of this new continent, effectively occurred after Columbus' discovery in 1492, not after the discovery by the Vikings. In both cases, we could assess the impact of each respective discovery only centuries later. It was almost impossible to predict at the time it was taking place, where each discovery would have led to.

C. This means that when people living in future times will look back on what you call this extraordinary revolution taking place right now, they may figure out it wasn't so important as you're telling me and maybe less important than other revolutions driven by technology.

P. For sure, people living a long time ahead of us in the future will be in a better position to judge it than we are, but some features which are intrinsic to our present revolution, by themselves alone allow us to understand that we're undoubtedly at a turning point in history, in terms of the ways we receive information and communicate with others.

Today's smartphones and social media are showing us how, for the first time in history, the evolution of communication technology has accelerated and overtaken at blinding speed our biological evolution as a species.

C. What do you exactly mean by this?

P. As an example, if you take any human being who lived a few thousand years ago and compare it to any other human being living today, their respective biological evolutions barely differ.

However, there's a massive difference between the way they communicated in the past, including the more recent past, when using traditional landline phones, versus today by video-call, with the capability of sending message attachments in the same call. An extraordinary change in so short a period of time. It appears like something totally normal today, while it would have appeared almost unthinkable one century ago.

For the first time in history, most people in the world can literally carry in their pockets a device which gives them access to the largest amount of information ever available in multiple formats, whether written, sound or video. How is this availability changing our lives? Does it improve it? Does it improve the learning capabilities and the quality of life of our younger generations? Does it improve our freedom, or does it rather increase control over us? In other words, where are we heading to, and how can we take control of these new means in order to safeguard our freedom?

C. Questions which seem difficult to answer.

P. Let's narrow our outlook and start considering how teens are impacted by smartphones, given the fact they make extensive use of them. Since I'm talking to you as a teen, I won't address an even more dreadful scenario concerning kids younger than you, who are grown on extensive smartphone usage. Focusing on teens alone, many of them spend hours of their day with their eyes stuck to their smartphones, so it's definitely worthwhile to ask if doing so improves the quality of their lives.

I will raise many red flags about the dangers of smartphone usage. By the way, these dangers may also concern other devices connected to the internet, such as computers and tablets. We prioritize smartphones in our considerations because of their ubiquity, diffusion and ease of access.

C. You're now implying smartphones wreak damage on teens, how can you prove it?

P. I'll focus more on this when talking about social media later on. Right now, I want to explain to you how the smartphone isn't designed to turn you into a free person, it's rather designed to control you. It's a subtle domination which you must learn to tackle.

By the way, since smartphones, that is, touchscreen phones with internet access, have by far and large replaced traditional cellular phones, from here on I'll simply call phones what we actually intend as smartphones.

C. It's difficult for me to fully realize I'm dominated, as you say, the moment I use my phone.

P. I'll explain to you how every phone user is relentlessly targeted at all times by the tech companies whose software is installed on phones. It's an invisible non-stop attack aimed at controlling each phone user.

There are different degrees of control a phone can have over you. Before being controlled, you are monitored. In first place, you're monitored by your phone. This means that any action taken on your phone is followed by others.

C. Who monitors me on my phone?

P. Many different agents, to call them in an unbiased way, monitor you the moment you turn on your phone. Actually, you can be monitored even if your phone is turned off, in case special software known as spyware is installed on your phone.

Let's start from the operating system which is the engine making your phone work. Just to take the two most popular ones, Android and iOs, the moment you turn on your phone, and it connects to the internet, a massive amount of data is sent to the one of those two companies whose operating system is running on your phone.

C. What do they monitor exactly?

P. They monitor as much data as possible pertaining to the activity of your phone. When we say the activity of our phones is monitored, this means that information referred to as data is continuously collected. By doing so, the parties who collect data maintain a dynamic view of what's going on in your phone. Far from being like a static picture, a dynamic picture is collected thanks to the continuous flow of data through the internet, which provides updated information on the status of the phone.

C. How about phone apps?

P. They do just the same. Collected data is essential in order to perform control. No matter how they sell you the idea that monitoring is required to enhance the performance of a device or an app, it ultimately serves the purpose of having under control the user of that device.

C. How can you actually know your phone is sending out that information?

P. I'll give you a down-to-earth example. The moment you turn on a phone and connect it to the internet, it will start shooting out data to different receiving entities.

I did the test myself. I purchased a cheap standard phone and intercepted its internet traffic. What I did was use another device as a tap which captured the flow of data which originated from my phone. After several minutes, I stopped my capture and checked it. I found that my phone had established connections to over two hundred different IP addresses.

C. What's an IP address?

P. To make it simple, just like individuals have a phone number where they can be reached at, an IP address is a number assigned to the point of access a certain device has on the internet. Therefore, an IP address is also assigned to your phone's point of access to the internet. Just like two individuals chat over the phone through their respective phone numbers, data is transferred between your phone and a receiving device on the other end through their respective IP addresses.

C. What does that data look like?

P. A lot of it is encrypted. The information is scrambled into gibberish which is managed only by the two devices at each end of the established connection. Encryption guarantees the secrecy of the communication, so no third party can eavesdrop on it, but it also prevents the phone user to understand it while it takes place, unless another device is set up to intercept that traffic and decrypt it.

C. Do you mean to say information from our phone is taken out without our consent?

P. Companies who install software on your phone should inform you about what information they collect. The bottom line is that you don't really see what data is sent. The subtle thing is, that since you don't physically see the millions of data bytes which your phone is sending out at all times, you are led to believe no communication is taking place, aside from the communication you think you're in control of at the moment.

Say you have an active connection with a certain website. You are led to believe that connection is the only active one, while the fact of the matter is your phone may have many other open connections at the same time, which are totally invisible to you.

C. This means that I can't realize how much information is actually sent between my phone and whatever parties on the other end?

P. That is so. Unless you painstakingly employ devices and software, separately from your phone, in order to intercept, or capture, which is the technical term pertaining to this operation, all of that invisible flow of data.

C. How about if I decided to capture the flow of data generated by my phone to and from the internet?

P. The cost is trivial. All you need is a decent enough computer or laptop, just like many you find on the market. You'll also need free software which will record and store that data, and basic networking equipment. You would need to operate this capture within any environment which allows you to place the capturing equipment in a handy enough way, such as a home or an office. You could even do it outdoors, even if less practical.

This allows you to capture virtually every single byte of data your phone is sending and receiving.

C. Once I capture all this data, what does it look like?

P. Here's where you need a solid technical knowledge of computer networking protocols in order to understand that data. In case you don't have the specific skills required to understand it, you'll need to rely on someone who has those skills.

Just as an example, if you were to capture data traffic generated by your phone while browsing the internet, streaming some video or updating the phone's software, you may easily build up a file greater than one gigabyte in just a few minutes. Considering all this captured data is in the shape of separate packets usually smaller than fifteen hundred bytes each, you could easily have to analyze over one million of those individual packets just for a short capture.

C. I can't even fathom the idea of analyzing all that data.

P. To be true, if you're familiar with this type of analysis, it's fairly straightforward. Of course, you need the expertise to do it.

This is precisely what analysts of Citizen Lab did. Citizen Lab is an organization which is part of the University of Toronto, Canada. They analyzed data traffic from compromised phones owned by political dissidents. They published detailed reports proving how spyware had been installed on those phones upon opening content received by email.

Those phones were "calling home", so to speak, basically sending out confidential information contained in the compromised phones, to rogue servers around the world, where those rogue servers were the spyware's home.

C. You mentioned phone users today, in 2025, are almost sixty percent of the world's population, so we're talking about five billion people. How many of those five billion would care to check what data their phones are sending or receiving?

P. I'd guess less than 0.1%. This means that likely over 99.9% of phone users worldwide have no idea about what data their device is sending and receiving at all times.

Think about it for a moment: five billion phones generating traffic which is for the most part unknown to the owners of those phones.

Here I need to emphasize once again the uniqueness of this technological revolution mankind is going through for the first time in history. Five billion people carry in their pockets the most important communication device ever available, and they have no idea of the actual data their phone is sending and receiving, which is far more than what they can see on their screen.

C. Where's the uniqueness of today's phones, versus other technological inventions like traditional phones, cars, planes?

P. As I see it, today's phones are essentially different from those other inventions, not because today's phones are more or less sophisticated, or because they're more or less useful, which is something I wouldn't start debating now.

The real difference lies in the degree of control and potential manipulation today's phones exert on us.

When you consider traditional landline phones, they're essentially conduits allowing verbal communications between people, carrying words like in face-to-face conversations. They aren't designed to pull out our confidential or personal information.

The same holds true for cars and planes which are designed to take us from one place to another. Once their transportation function is carried out, they don't retain control over us.

C. What you're saying is that for the first time in history a device is structured to keep the population under control?

P. Yes. Let me clarify a bit here. Even if people may say today's phones are simply an enhanced version of traditional phones, they're not at all. They created and are creating a whole new dimension for mankind.

This dimension allows an unprecedented degree of control which we don't perceive and also allows new forms of manipulation, as I will explain to you later when talking about social media.

In order to understand the radical changes brought about by today's phones, we must consider how they impact the primitive biological nature of human beings.

Recalling my example of the three-hundred-yard-long wall encompassing the history of mankind, I showed you how today's phones have been used so far for a period of time comparable to an inch along that distance.

As human beings, we originate from a very primitive environment, we were all basically apes who then developed into what we are now, but our physical and mental structure have retained primitive mechanisms which drive our reactions, for example when we perceive a situation of danger. We are emotional beings.

C. Sorry, but I really can't see where you're taking me to, about the fact we developed out of monkeys.

P. Hang on, I'm getting to the point.

Say you're on the side of a high-traffic road, and you need to cross it to reach the other side. Many cars pass along the road until you see no more cars at close range, so you start crossing the road at a normal pace, but all of a sudden, another car enters the road and speeds up toward you. At that point, you frantically dash forward to prevent that car from running you down.

This example shows your phylogenetic structure at work: just like a monkey would have leaped forward to save its life, you do the same, because our senses are triggered to react when we perceive a danger is present.

C. What do you mean by "phylogenetic structure"?

P. I mean the biological structure we, as human beings, have inherited from our ape-like ancestors through evolution. Our survival instinct is a built-in feature of our biological structure.

Now I have to go back to my previous description of the flow of data between your phone and the internet: it's about millions of data bytes racing at blinding speed from and to your phone across the air.

Those data bytes are like cars on a high-traffic road. However, with one main difference: your data bytes in the shape of zeros and ones, which is how data travel across cables or through the air, are invisible, you don't see them. All you see is the screen of your phone.

C. I fail to see the meaning of this comparison.

P. Let me complete my explanation by starting to focus on the big picture. For the first time in the history of mankind, the greater part of human beings lives with a device which is constantly sending and receiving a massive amount of information in the shape of invisible digital units.

This process lies completely undetected by our senses. Our biological structure doesn't allow us to perceive it. Therefore, it can't generate any sense of danger, like instead cars moving on a road we're standing close to.

The only way we can see the danger of this flow of information is by conceptualizing it. This means I can't rely on my built-in instinctual structure. The danger I can understand about my phone sending out details about myself such as my current geographical location, as well as any other personal and private information, stems from my intellective reasoning, not from my senses which are left untouched by the invisible flow of information.

C. I don't feel concerned because I literally don't see the amount of information my phone is sending out. My instincts can't be triggered by a danger I can't see.

P. Correct. In my example, you found yourself in the middle of the road believing cars had passed, but a new car popped out, triggering your instinctive reaction to immediately move out of the way. Here are your senses at work. Your reaction to save your life is the same which was at work in those apes which gradually developed into human beings. Those senses preserved our species.

Let's compare the danger of the car running you down, to the danger of all your confidential information being stolen off your phone through some rogue connection.

You see the former, not the latter. Your senses are unaffected by whatever information leaves your phone without your consent, simply because you don't see it.

Therefore, I can seek protection from being controlled only through my free-thinking capacity. My primitive sensorial structure which serves the purpose of self-preservation against danger, will not help me.

In order to prevent my personal information from being fed to some tech company, I'll have to restrict the capabilities of my phone by changing its settings, by not installing social media apps and so on.

C. Which is probably why the current five billion phone users around the globe have no worries about being controlled through their phones. Eye doesn't see, heart doesn't hurt.

P. Exactly. The power of an intellective argument proving you're in danger still fails against its lack of evidence gathered by your basic senses.

Nevertheless, we can't accept the idea that human beings across the globe want to become numbers within a digital system or part of a mass of useful idiots created by social media, as I'll explain later.

We want to hope our present conversation reaches the greatest possible amount of people, so our readers can ponder over what I'm about to say.

C. Are you implying you can bring strong enough reasons to get people off their phones worldwide?

P. That's not my goal. Today's phones are useful in many respects, just like many other technological devices. We don't want to go back to the Stone Age. But, remember, our concern is to raise awareness over being controlled and manipulated.

Let me be clear on this. The phone itself is not the problem. The problem is how it's designed by human beings. A knife can be used to cut tomatoes in half, but it can also be used to kill a person.

Gutenberg invented the printing press in the fifteenth century in what is now Germany. This invention triggered the distribution of books across Europe. Many people could finally read the Bible printed in multiple copies. However, that same invention gave rise to witch-hunting manuals which expanded the witch-hunt craze causing the death of thousands of alleged witches, who were innocent people in most cases.

C. Where is the danger we can't see in our phones?

P. I'll first get a bit more technical, thereafter I will illustrate a scenario which will help to explain.

By what I described earlier, we know that our phone sends out massive amounts of data. We know that all this data is invisible, and the only way to see it is to capture it through some external device such as a computer with appropriate software which will store all that data traffic for us in a file.

A popular free software which serves this purpose is Wireshark. Thanks to its extensive variety of settings, it allows us to analyze network traffic in depth. There are other useful free software tools called HTTP proxies which also allow you to analyze the invisible data flow generated by your phone. In order to make the best out of these tools, a deep knowledge of network protocols is required, and we certainly can't expect our current five billion phone users to master it.

For that matter, we want to offer a shortcut explanation to our five billion phone users in order to see what's going on inside their phones.

C. Sounds like an extremely ambitious task.

P. It is, but all I want to provide is a visual idea of the process.

Let me explain: we said that our phone is shooting out data at all times, so five billion users are invisibly reporting to various receiving entities who they are, where they are, what's going on inside their phones and so forth.

C. Who are these receiving entities?

P. The companies providing the phone's operating system, for example Apple or Alphabet (the company who owns Google), any app provider, social media companies, your mobile phone carrier, anyone behind installed software or spyware, including the government. By the way, this last situation is very common in countries with authoritarian governments who invest significant financial resources to spy on any political opponent.

All this flow of information is absolutely real, but it's invisible.

C. Thanks to software like Wireshark, we know that every single one of today's five billion phones, is spitting out a bunch of hidden information to many receiving entities.

P. Correct. Now, I want to imagine a hypothetical scenario which is too good to be true. It would be in the shape of an imaginary privacy-oriented app where each user would be informed in real time about the invisible traffic going on in her phone, like a simplified, user-friendly version of Wireshark where different types of data would appear like thin horizontal colored lines covering the top part of the screen, thus resizing a bit the screen content and making it slightly smaller in order to allow those colored lines to be visible at all times.

Just like we see cars dashing in front of us on a highway, each car has a different color. By the same token, we would assign a different color to each type of data which is sent and received by our phone to and from the internet.

C. According to this imaginary scenario, I would be physically seeing different colored lines on the top part the phone's screen, where each color would indicate a specific type of data.

P. Not only. In this scenario, we would want each colored line to contain information pertaining to the sending and receiving parties of the data. By tapping on each colored line, the phone user would also see where the information is coming from or going to. Tiny arrows would indicate whether that traffic is incoming or outgoing.

This idea is typical of software firewalls, which are programs designed to monitor and control computer-generated data traffic. In our case, I want to imagine it as an interface on your phone's screen, which can be easily understood by the average phone user.

C. How would the information inside each colored line look like?

P. We would want it accurate, but also user-friendly, that is, understandable by anyone who has no technical knowledge of network protocols or software.

Let's assume a black-colored line would indicate data is being received or sent by one of the phone's browsers. This would tell the user when the browser is sending or receiving data, even when the browser isn't active on the phone's screen.

The information accessed by tapping on the colored line would tell the user which IP addresses correspond to the endpoints of the live communication and would provide additional technical information pertaining to that communication. By endpoints I mean where the data comes from and goes to, between your phone's IP address and the IP address on the opposite end. This could get a bit technical, but at least would allow some users to get curious and try to better understand what's going on behind the screen.

As an example, when you access a popular webpage, say a news site, what you see on your screen is in most cases pulled out from multiple IP addresses almost at the same time. Often, well over a dozen IP addresses are accessed in a fraction of a second.

This fact by itself would crowd the app with a huge amount of information, the moment a user would decide to drill down and see what's going on under the hood.

C. What other colored lines would appear when the phone is connected to the internet?

P. For example, a green line would indicate that software updates are being checked or downloaded.

By seeing these multiple colored lines at the same time, one on top of the other, the user would start becoming aware of the different types of traffic generated by the phone in the background.

While each user believes to be normally browsing or streaming any known content, there are several other types of packets entering and exiting the phone which the user would never be aware of, unless we assume our fictitious scenario allowed us to see them in different colors.

C. Would you consider a lot more colored lines?

P. Yes, a few more for sure.

A purple-colored line would show data sent and received through apps. By tapping on the purple line, the user would gather information about which apps are generating data traffic, even when they aren't active on the phone's screen.

An orange-colored line would show data being sent and received by the phone's operating system, not including software updates which we referred to earlier, when we assigned to them a green-colored line.

The most important colored line would be the red one, indicating that confidential personal information or information which identifies the phone user, is being sent out. When tapping on the red line, any information which identifies the user or the phone, regardless of which app or location in the phone's storage it gets pulled out from, would be displayed in the clear to the user. Ideally, we would want a beeping sound to go along with it in order to enhance the sense of alert.

In our imaginary scenario, our privacy-oriented app would be smart enough to figure out when any information pertaining to the user or the phone and its settings is sent out, allowing the user to have all possible information about the receiving party.

I could carry on assigning more colors to other types of data, but I think you got the idea, right?

C. Yes. Basically you would want people to see in real time the different types of data generated by their phone, so they could assess the nature of the invisible traffic which their device is relentlessly creating.

P. Now, let me ask you a question about our hypothetical scenario. You see a red-colored line on the top of your screen, and you know it reflects your personal and private information including, for example, your date of birth and home address, as well as usernames, passwords, preferences, chosen apps, browsing history, private email messages, etc.

You are just one of our five billion current phone users, and by tapping on that red line you would be able to see in real time the exact information your phone is throwing out about yourself, and where it is going to.

Let's assume you can read the name of the party who's receiving your confidential data, whether it's the company whose operating system is on your phone, whether it's a specific social media app, or whether it's some rogue server around the world.

Well, these things really happen at all times on your phone, as we know by analyzing its traffic with the specific tools we described earlier.

My question to you is: how would you feel when all the previously invisible traffic becomes visible, alerting you at any given moment about what type of data your phone is sending out? How would you feel if you could physically see in real time your most intimate information being released through the internet? How would you feel if you could read at any given moment a list of personal identifying data your phone is spitting out at all times?

C. I'd think: why the heck is all this personal information of mine pulled out without me having control over when and how this occurs?

P. The simple fact of seeing it would alarm you, right?

It won't alarm you the moment you are entering your username and password to access a certain service online, because you know that's exactly what you're doing at that moment in time, but it certainly would scare you when the red-colored alert pops out while you're not taking any such action on your phone.

I previously illustrated to you how a car popping out and speeding toward you while you're crossing a road, would immediately activate your senses to run out of the car's way.

By the same token, if you were to see in plain sight a red line on the top of your phone's screen, labeled with extremely confidential information you aren't intentionally sending to anyone, but is leaving your phone directed to some unidentified receiver on the internet, you would instantly panic, asking yourself why that data is leaving your phone when it's not supposed to.

C. The same idea could be applied to health conditions. Someone may not worry at all about having some mild symptoms, until an MRI exam traces those symptoms to cancer. Knowledge is the key, and invisible information is like no information.

P. I couldn't have said it any better.

As a starting point, the hypothetical scenario of visualizing private information which is stolen from phone users would make those users aware of this.

C. Would it be possible to enforce this alerting system on all phones worldwide?

P. It would be an extremely complex endeavor.

One challenge in building such an app would be the underlying operating system, and we know that almost all phones today run on either Android or iOS.

C. Why would that be a problem?

P. The two corporations owning those two operating systems would still be the ones in control of your phone and could easily decide to disable your privacy-oriented app with a software update, up to the point of pretending to treat it like a security vulnerability.

I'll give you an example on a different matter which however illustrates the point.

I installed a VPN app on my Mac notebook. Thereafter, I captured my internet traffic to see if it was all funnelled through my VPN tunnel.

C. What's a VPN?

P. In basic terms, a VPN, which stands for Virtual Private Network, is a connection working through a specific type of software installed on your device which encrypts and funnels all your internet traffic to a dedicated computer server on the internet, which becomes your effective point of access to the internet. The virtual and private network is the space between your device and your remote point of access to the internet. Any IP address to which you connect will see the VPN server's IP address instead of seeing your real IP address from where you start the connection, thus hiding your real IP address.

C. What did you notice about your internet traffic going through the VPN?

P. I noticed that it wasn't going all through the VPN, as it was supposed to. Many data packets were still sent directly to Apple servers, bypassing my VPN connection, even if it was designed to funnel my entire traffic to and through a single VPN server.

C. Therefore, our privacy-oriented app would have to be in control of your operating system.

P. Not only. Aside from your phone's software and hardware, there are two more areas you would have to be in control of, before considering you have your private information secured and not leaked.

This is where we have to pay our immense tribute to a few people, namely whistleblowers, whom I'll soon talk to you about.

The first area is the internet itself. Whistleblowers have clearly shown how the U.S. government has a granular control over it.

Regardless of your privacy-oriented app telling you what type of data your phone is sending out, the government will see your online activity on the internet.

The second area are social media companies, whose secretive management and intrusive mechanisms have also been uncovered by whistleblowers.

Again, even if your privacy-oriented app tells you what data you're sending out through your social media app, you won't be able to see how your personal data is managed by the social media company, and how it gets weaponized against you to feed you the contents it shoots back at you, because this entire process takes place behind the closed doors of that company, as I'll explain to you very soon.

C. How is it possible for phones to monitor their users on a general scale? How can this be allowed?

P. The phone is designed as an interface between its user and different systems. What I generically call systems are all the entities which consistently and relentlessly pull out out data from your phone. These entities take data from your operating system, your apps and other software installed on your phone. Each phone user is functional to the survival of these entities, call them Android, iOS or any other app.

These entities haven't been designed having in mind your well-being. All of them are structured according to a business model. We'll see this very well later on, when addressing social media, where social media are structured to keep you engaged as much as possible, up to the point of making you a sheer addict of their algorithms.

C. This still doesn't answer my question. Why is all this allowed?

P. We'll get into this later. I'll show you how the invisible nature of data being transferred to and from your phone allows companies to spy on you and to manipulate you, and how political authorities lag behind in keeping this state of things under control.

Another reason why this is allowed, is that many people don't care. They don't care to be monitored and tracked on everything they're doing on their phones. This is mostly out of ignorance, as I explained about people ignoring the extent of their being exploited as phone users.

However, there are notable people who do care. For example, the great software programmer Richard Stallman lives without a phone, so nobody can use that device to track him.

C. I would guess very few people have that approach. How can you reduce or limit this monitoring activity?

P. You can certainly take significant measures to reduce the amount of monitoring, but let's call it by its real name, the amount of spying of which you're the target.

There are many ways for you to greatly limit the amount of spying by tech companies which operate in the background of your phone. For example, you can use free operating systems as well as apps which greatly reduce your exposure. By using operating systems and apps designed with the clear intent of safeguarding your privacy, you greatly reduce the monitoring activity targeted at you.

C. Where can I find information telling me how I can protect myself from the spying activity which phones are subject to?

P. I will dedicate the following part of our conversation to this issue. I will focus on the revelations from whistleblowers who allowed us to understand how control and manipulation of phone users are carried out. By understanding how this happens, you'll understand how you can protect yourself consequently.

Before we get into that, I want you to know about two fantastic YouTubers who dedicate a huge amount of effort in educating people on the vulnerabilities of their devices. They address your question in many of their videos.

One is Naomi Brockwell. She's based in Australia. You'll find many of her videos are extremely useful, in terms of explaining how you can effectively restrict any spying activity you're subject to, as a phone or computer user.

The other is David Bombal. He's based in the UK.

Both of them occasionally invite experts to explain these matters.

C. I will check them out for sure.

So, basically, the way I use my phone is analyzed in order to control me?

P. Ultimately, yes. The companies who design operating systems and apps need to have as much data as possible about what is happening on your phone. The ultimate goal of that software is to acquire power over its users. The power of tech companies who control phones or devices which connect to the internet goes beyond controlling single user profiles. It controls billions of people at the same time.

By the same token, search results on the web are filtered and selected along the interests of the search engine you use. The same happens for news which pop-up on your favorite app or home page. The tech company which provides news to you, will filter and manipulate them according to its own political and economic interests.

C. Therefore, I should approach that news which has been selected for me, considering it doesn't randomly appear, asking myself why it's displayed in a certain way, just like you explained earlier about the news in general.

P. The process of selecting news and presenting it in a certain way on your phone is similar to what we described about the news being broadcast through TV channels, the radio, newspapers, etc.

With one very significant difference, however. On a phone you are literally interacting with the news you're reading or watching. You tap your screen here and there, selecting the information you're fed, and the device which gives that information records your reaction to it, stores the information you're feeding it and processes it, updating furthermore your individual profile and acquiring more elements which will serve the purpose of manipulating you even more.

Watching the news on TV is essentially a unidirectional flow of information from the TV to the user who is a passive recipient of information. The danger of the bidirectional flow of information on a phone where users constantly interact with the news, is that users provide a massive wealth of information about themselves, which is elaborated to enhance the capabilities of control and manipulation by whoever has access to your phone data.

C. Since well over half of the world's population uses phones, this means that most human beings today are controlled, or at worst, manipulated by the companies whose software is on their phones?

P. It is so, definitely. Today we are far more aware of this than we were when the first internet-connected phones came around, thanks to some real heroes who had the morals and guts to come out and inform the world about the exploitation and manipulation of internet-connected device users, primarily phone users.

Whistleblowers

C. You said: heroes?

P. Sure, whistleblowers.

C. Who's a whistleblower?

P. A whistleblower is a person within an organization where unethical or illegal activities take place, who decides to report these activities to others inside the organization or to the public, often at the risk of her own life. The decision of reporting these activities in order to raise awareness in people, is referred to as "blowing the whistle".

There are different types of whistleblowers, depending on the type of organization they work or have worked for. These organizations can be either public or private. They can be government entities like the army, or private companies like an oil corporation.

For our present matter, we narrow down the concept to define an individual who reports unethical or illegal activities carried out by a large organization, through internet-connected devices, mostly phones, and social media.

All the whistleblowers I'll name in our conversation are critical thinkers. Their actions have enlightened our knowledge and awareness of the manipulation we're all subject to, as phone and social media users.

These whistleblowers are revolutionary in a way which is totally new in history.

C. Are you telling me we can't find anyone like them in the past?

P. It is precisely so. It's the very first time in history dissent appears in this shape.

C. What makes their dissent so unique?

P. Before replying to your question, I want to give you a quick overview of dissent in the course of history.

We've seen the wide-ranging effects of dissent at many levels: political, religious, social, economic, scientific, artistic and so on.

Our focus is on dissent driven by critical thinking.

Just to name a few, we can think of Jesus Christ as a major dissenter within Judaism. Luther was the same within the Catholic Church.

Galileo Galilei, considered by many as the father of modern physics and astronomy, was a dissenter in his own right, as his scientific views were fiercely opposed by the Catholic Church of his time, four centuries ago.

Looking back at the last century and bearing in mind a broad idea of dissent, physicist and mathematician Albert Einstein dissented from some scientific concepts of his time, and artist Marcel Duchamp reshaped the idea of art, amongst other things, by flipping over a urinal and giving it the dignity of an art work.

We could carry on and on with many more examples showing how some individuals detached themselves from the mindset of their contemporaries. Yet, no matter how many cases of dissent we may pull out from history, nothing is even by far comparable to the action of the whistleblowers we are taking into consideration. This takes me back to your question about what makes their dissent so unique.

C. You're making me even more curious about whistleblowers.

P. What makes them so unique lies in the unprecedented features of today's communication of data on the internet where, both the government and companies with overwhelming online presence, can control billions of people through their devices.

I showed you how the internet and internet-capable phones or devices came around on a large scale no more than three decades ago, and how this allowed online systems to collect granular data on the population and to exert control over it. By online systems, I mean state-owned or private organizations having online presence and control.

For the first time in history, most of the world's population can be tracked and controlled in the finest detail by a technocratic elite within newly formed systems having a pervasive online presence, without the world population being aware of the nature of this control.

These technological conditions have triggered a totally new type of dissent represented by whistleblowers. This type of dissent has brought to our attention the alarming threats of the technocratic society we live in, where a few people control the rest of the population through the invisible and intrusive use of technology, in a way which is very difficult to detect.

A few individuals working within those online systems, turned into whistleblowers, thus allowing the population to understand the dangers to individual freedom posed by those same systems.

C. How should we categorize today's whistleblowers you are referring to? Should we consider them political dissenters?

P. They are, in terms of being opponents of a system of power. However, they don't reflect the classical definition of a political dissenter, often referred to as a dissident.

Dissidents typically stem from authoritarian political systems, such as those of the Soviet Union and post-Soviet Russia. Just to mention a recent case, out of a very long list of dissidents murdered in that country, Alexei Navalny died last year after having spent his life opposing the Russian authoritarian regime.

The remarkable feature of our whistleblowers, is that they originate from the system of power they oppose, not from the population targeted by that same system of power. Political groups in the government may change, however power through technology remains.

Given the continuous progress of technology, we are led to believe our whistleblowers are likely the first of many more to come, which is a scary perspective, to say the least.

C. Therefore, power over people is no more exercised by political authorities alone, it's also carried out by tech companies whose activity is based on technology.

P. Yes, changes in the traditional structure of power followed the diffusion of phones and the internet as we explained, especially in the last two decades.

Boundaries between politics and technology are fading away. This reminds me of societies without a clear separation of politics and religion. Paradoxically, it's like jumping back in history by one thousand years, in the Middle Ages, when the Catholic Church compounded both political and religious authorities. Or like the Iranian present-day regime, where the Ayatollah holds both political and religious authorities.

C. Technology like a new form of religion?

P. Let me first draw a distinction.

On the one hand, when power relies on religion, it claims it has a metaphysical foundation. In short, taking my examples of the Catholic Church in the Middle Ages and today's Iranian regime, power claims it is the expression of the will of God.

On the other hand, when power relies on technology, it doesn't claim technology is the reason of its existence. Technology is rather the tool used by power to achieve its goals.

Lo and behold: as of today, I'm ruling out the horrifying scenario where technology develops to the point of becoming a thinking entity in its own right and takes power over human beings. This scenario can be envisaged with the development of artificial intelligence.

C. Why then would you liken technology to religion in its relationship to power?

P. I liken them in terms of their instrumental function. Just like power uses religion to sway people's minds, it uses technology for the same purpose. However, the way technology is used to manipulate people is far more subtle.

When power uses religious arguments to justify its decisions, it does so in an open way. People may or may not agree with those decisions and their being justified by religion, but the message given by power is clear. The message is: follow my orders because I am the word of God.

On the other hand, thanks to our whistleblowers, we know technology is used to manipulate people in an ever-increasing surreptitious way, bypassing people's awareness.

C. Who are the whistleblowers we should thank for having raised awareness in people?

P. I first need to draw another distinction on two different types of whistleblowers we're taking into consideration.

The first type stems from state-owned entities, and brings to light the hidden surveillance activities of such entities. Whistleblowers working within these state-owned entities have shown, specifically in the U.S., how a granular collection of personal and private data pertaining to all individual citizens, is carried out without the consent of the citizens themselves and even without the explicit authorization of Congress, which is at the heart of the U.S. political power.

The second type of whistleblowers stems from corporations known as social media platforms. Whistleblowers within these entities, have shown how personal and private data of users of social media platforms serve the purpose of controlling and manipulating those same users, up to the point of influencing their behavior and their choices in everyday life, without those users being aware of it.

C. Which of these two types of whistleblowers will you describe?

P. I'll describe both types of whistleblowers. You'll see how they all share common traits, including the fact they have been or are still active in the last three decades, when we saw the growing rise of the internet and internet-capable phones.

I'll now start off with the first type, the ones who worked within state-owned entities.

We can set a milestone back in 2002 when several NSA officials openly argued against the intrusiveness of the NSA, or National Security Agency, which is part of the U.S. Department of Defense. The growing internet was becoming a handy way for the government to pull out massive amounts of confidential data regarding the population.

Their revelations started an eye-opening process focused on the misuse and abuse of power through technology.

Just over ten years later, in 2013, when the technological capabilities of the NSA had furthermore expanded, Edward Snowden came around with even more impactful revelations which immediately spread worldwide.

C. Who is Edward Snowden?

P. Edward Snowden is a computer and cybersecurity expert who worked for the CIA and also as an NSA contractor. In June 2013, he started revealing to the world how the American government was spying on all of its citizens, as well as on other countries, by leveraging its control on all means of communication, primarily the internet and phones.

Snowden explained in great detail how U.S. government agencies, specifically the NSA, have granular access to the private information of all citizens, and how all this information is stored in massive databases, without informing citizens about this.

He also explained how government agencies access private online information of citizens such as phone, email and social media communications, without requesting consent.

In one word, Snowden explained to the world the fakeness of privacy, by proving how the government can virtually access whatever it wants from a citizen without any warrant in place.

Utterly disgusted by seeing all this going on while he was working within those agencies, and having no success in steering his co-workers and supervisors against such practices, he understood the only way to undermine the system was to reveal this state of things to the press, and therefore, to the world, by providing detailed documentary evidence.

C. Snowden's new type of dissent points to an alarming threat which was never present in the past?

P. Yes, though I would also include his predecessors at the NSA in this new type of dissent which tells us how today's society is structured.

Opposition against any system of power usually stemmed from a well-known threat or constraint. Before June 2013, when Snowden's revelations had a worldwide impact, people who expressed their dissent against an oppressive system of power wouldn't be regarded as a surprise, because the general public was aware of the wrongdoings of that system. On top of this, political dissenters would often originate not from the controlling elite or from the privileged dominating class. They would rather originate from dominated classes or groups.

Restricting our considerations to the last century, all dissenters within communist or fascist societies were seen by their contemporary citizens, as individuals who were challenging a clear threatening power.

This type of dissent is still very present in many societies and countries, as we speak.

C. What are the features of whistleblowers like Snowden, as opposed to the traditional political dissenters you described?

P. The new type of dissent brought by whistleblowers like Snowden is the product of today's technocratic society, where political or financial power uses technology in order to achieve its goals.

The actions of the whistleblowers I will tell you about, are a very clear result of critical thinking. These individuals worked within companies whose main target is to control and manipulate millions, if not billions, of people.

By critically analyzing the purpose of their own work, our whistleblowers determined to quit their activities within those organizations or companies and to inform the general public of the wrongdoings of those organizations or companies.

C. Do these whistleblowers have common traits?

P. They certainly do. You may almost think of a stereotype.

The whistleblower we are talking about is a highly intelligent individual with advanced skills and technical competence in her field of operation.

The whistleblower operates within the structure which exerts its power over people who don't dwell within that structure. The crucial point to bear in mind is that the source of dissent coincides with the source of power, not with the target of that same power.

C. What do you exactly mean when you say "the source of dissent coincides with the source of power"?

P. I'll explain it with an example.

Let's take the French Revolution of 1789. The source of power was the aristocracy, that is, the king and his affiliates. The source of dissent against that power was within the population who was subdued by that power.

The source of dissent against the ruling class didn't originate from that same class. It originated from the oppressed classes.

The remarkable feature about all our whistleblowers, is that they originate from the ruling class, so to speak, not from the oppressed classes.

The uniqueness of this condition, where dissent originates within the source of power, tells us how secret and closed to the public are the inner workings of these structures, where an extremely small number of people is fully aware of the amount of control and manipulation carried out against billions of totally unaware people.

The people who are controlled and manipulated by technology which is weaponized against them, don't realize they are being exploited, hence their group doesn't generate individuals who push for a revolt.

C. Since these whistleblower revelations originated from within those secretive structures of power, can we say that without whistleblowers the public wouldn't have known about this control and manipulation of billions of people?

P. Yes, the role played by whistleblowers was and is absolutely crucial in undermining the use of technology aimed at controlling and manipulating billions of individuals.

However, this new type of dissent which uncovers the misuse and abuse of technology, doesn't originate exclusively from the source of technocratic power. It may also arise outside of the source of that power, but when this occurs, it's typically in the shape of academics or researchers who study the nefarious results of manipulation through technology, as I'll show later when dealing with social media.

The academic who criticizes the unethical use of technology, is very similar to the whistleblower in the fact that, even if not an insider, is typically a highly intelligent and competent individual, who discerns the nature of exploitation through technology and the consequent damage to the victims of that exploitation.

C. By what you're saying, it appears that only highly competent individuals within the tech industry, or highly educated people like academics or researches, have uncovered the abuse of technology, in place of the victims of such abuse doing so. So far you haven't mentioned one victim of the system revolting against it. Does this mean that critical thinking is a rare quality restricted to highly competent or educated people?

P. Should I reply "yes" to your question, this would kill the whole purpose of my conversation with you, since I explained that critical thinking is a method anyone can make use of, aimed at reaching conclusions after having thoroughly analyzed the issues at stake, in an unbiased way, by setting individual freedom of thought and action as its ultimate goal.

Therefore, my reply to your question about critical thinking as being restricted to highly competent and educated people, is a big "no".

Higher education always helps, but applying the method I explained to you requires inquisitive reasoning and unbiased thinking which are essential, regardless of your education degree.

That said, the uniqueness of this type of dissent is that the whistleblower isn't the tip of the iceberg representing the population, who is supposed to be aware of being controlled and exploited.

The alarming concern is that dissent against online intrusion and social media, doesn't originate from the victimized population, proving once more that the victims don't perceive the threats to their individual freedom.

This type of contemporary dissent against technology-based structures of power, is characterized by a few whistleblowers operating on the controlling side, who tell the vast majority on the other, controlled side, that they are the ones being controlled and manipulated.

C. Given the importance of knowing the inner workings of these new structures of power, it's like as if critical thinking isn't enough by itself, because control and manipulation are carried out in a highly sophisticated way which can be understood only through advanced technological competence.

P. This is where we can take advantage of critical thinking from others, namely our whistleblowers. We, as critical thinkers, must be curious, inquisitive, and must analyze all the information we can gather from others.

Therefore, even if a critical thinker may have limited technological competence, she welcomes the information provided by whistleblowers and applies the method of questioning and analyzing that information in order to determine its truthfulness.

C. What today's whistleblowers are telling us, is that very few individuals who are in control of what is going on behind our phones, have a huge amount of power on billions of phone users.

P. Yes. We can safely say that, for the first time in history, an extremely small number of people has a huge amount of power on the global population, rather than only within single countries or areas.

The danger of this state of things isn't just about its extension, it's even more about the fact that this danger is invisible, as it conceals itself behind content which appears to be legitimate. The fact of allowing people to chat on social media gives the illusion that everyone can have her say, but this isn't the case, as we'll soon see when delving into the inner workings of social media.

Snowden came out in June 2013, reporting the depth of surveillance on all citizens, applied by government agencies through the internet and internet-capable devices. That same year was like a starting date for more whistleblowers to follow, reporting how social media control and manipulate billions of people.

C. Who are these other whistleblowers?

P. I'll now focus on the second type of whistleblowers who originate from large online corporations, most notably social media platforms.

First and foremost, Tristan Harris.

In 2013, just a few months before Snowden's revelations, Tristan Harris published a slide deck at Google, where he worked for three years. In that presentation he blows the whistle on how the tech giant was capturing users' attention, which points to one of the main objectives of social media, that is, to keep users engaged as much as possible.

We'll delve into these matters soon, when addressing how social media work, and why they have devastating effects on the minds of their users.

Suffice to say for now, that this was just one of the very first steps of Tristan Harris' relentless activity aimed at uncovering the subtle and surreptitious ways tech companies use to control and manipulate people.

Unlike other whistleblowers who uncovered the inner workings of tech companies and, thereafter, have been less visible to the public, Tristan Harris has been extremely active in his efforts to divulge to the public how tech companies, specifically social media, consistently manipulate their users up to the point of seriously impacting their mental health.

C. How is Tristan Harris carrying out his eye-opening activity?

P. In many ways.

He founded the Center for Humane Technology. Its website humanetech.com is an amazing source of information on the dangers of technology, and how technology can be reformed. It's extremely important in terms of indicating resources which are useful for understanding the misuse and abuse of technologies and also remedies for that matter.

He took part in the documentary "The Social Dilemma" which appeared in 2020, describing the inner workings of social media, and the mental damage caused by their use.

You can easily follow him on many online podcasts and also check his testimonies in Congress, which I will tell you about later.

C. Are there other whistleblowers you deem I should be aware of?

P. "The Social Dilemma" features several IT experts and academics who have studied the inner workings of social media.

I'll mention two IT experts, Aza Raskin and Guillaume Chaslot.

Aza Raskin worked at Mozilla Labs and Firefox. He invented the infinite scroll function and, with Tristan Harris, is a co-founder of the Center for Humane Technology. You can find several online conferences and podcasts of Tristan Harris and Aza Raskin together.

Guillaume Chaslot is a software engineer who worked at Google and founded the company AlgoTransparency.

Algotransparency.org is an extremely useful resource, in terms of explaining how algorithms are employed to manipulate social media users.

Another notable whistleblower is Christopher Wylie, a data analyst at a company named Cambridge Analytica, who, in March 2018, revealed to the world how the company he was working for, had collected detailed private information of eighty-seven million Facebook user accounts and had used that information to manipulate those users for political purposes.

I also have to mention Frances Haugen, who started her revelations in September 2021, specifically about Facebook, and Arturo Bejar, in November 2023, about Facebook and Instagram.

Like Tristan Harris, all these other whistleblowers played a crucial role in explaining to the world how the hidden structure behind our phone usage is designed to control and manipulate us. This hidden structure is made of entities which are secretive in nature and don't disclose their ways of operating. Therefore, it's extremely difficult for the general public to ever grasp the idea of how they effectively operate, unless someone from within those entities decides to come out and provide substantial documented evidence of unethical and illegal operations and methods.

C. This means that, if all these whistleblowers hadn't existed, the general population would have carried on without a clue about how they were manipulated.

P. It is so, notwithstanding the huge numbers of social media users: right now, Facebook counts over three billion users, and Instagram counts over two billion.

While Snowden had highlighted the intrusion carried out by state-owned entities, the other whistleblowers I mentioned, also highlighted the mental damage caused by social media.

Academics like Jonathan Haidt have proven the severity and diffusion of mental illness caused by social media.

Given the extension of mental damage within such a large population of users, it's remarkable to see how there was no spontaneous rebellion against social media.

In other words, the moment societies create conditions of oppression or exploitation, you normally see reactions from the bottom up, that is, from the base of the exploited individuals against the exploiting group.

In this respect, social media companies such as Facebook and Instagram have seen class actions or lawsuits which are ongoing.

However, these were triggered by revelations from whistleblowers who explained how users are manipulated, and how depression, anxiety and many other forms of mental illness are caused by extensive use of social media, especially among teens.

C. Therefore, these class actions weren't generated spontaneously by social media users. Whistleblowers preceded them, made those users aware they were being exploited and helped them understand the reasons behind the spread of mental illnesses among them.

P. Correct. What you just described, differs from the typical pattern of social revolts we see in history, where the exploited majority of the population at the bottom revolts against the exploiting minority at the top.

On the contrary, here we have people from the top, our whistleblowers who operated within the exploiting structures, making the people at the bottom aware of their condition of exploitation.

This fact by itself proves that the massive group of users exploited by social media as useful idiots, lacked the knowledge of our whistleblowers.

C. You're explaining this situation like a two-layered model: big tech corporations are the top layer, and the users of the products of those corporations are the bottom layer.

Even if the number of people in the top layer is just a tiny number, when compared to those in the bottom layer, I would still assume the ones in the top layer are many thousands, but the whistleblowers you mentioned are just over a handful of people.

How about all the other people in the top layer, who can witness the same things seen by our whistleblowers, and who instead keep on exploiting the people in the bottom layer?

P. The size and growth of these tech corporations, prove by themselves that the overwhelming majority of the people working for them, isn't making use of critical thinking. To be more specific, those people dedicate their lives to killing critical thinking.

We saw how critical thinking is finalized to enhance individual freedom of thought and action. The work of the employees of those corporations is instead finalized to kill freedom of thought and action.

When you consider all I told you so far, you'll notice how these whistleblowers and their personal histories represent a model of critical thinking.

By recalling what we said in previous parts of our conversation, all these whistleblowers don't fall prey of the sheep-effect, or what we described as the soccer-stadium-effect. They don't conform to the general behavior of co-workers or supervisors around them. They aren't afraid to question their employer, just like you shouldn't fear to question your school teacher. Their respective employers proved to be fully numb to their requests of change, which is why they were all left with no choice other than leaving their respective companies and revealing to the world the crimes they had witnessed. They analyzed the information they were fed, by adopting the method I explained to you and stuck to their own values avoiding to be manipulated.

These whistleblowers started their respective activities embracing in good faith the ideas of the companies they worked for. However, by gradually realizing the highly unethical nature of their job, they determined to refuse to play as useful idiots and turned into full-blown critical thinkers.

C. In a way, before becoming whistleblowers, they were also useful idiots like many others.

P. With the exception of Tristan Harris, who went straight to the point at Google where he worked as design ethicist, the other whistleblowers I mentioned started their careers working on the exploiting side, proving what I told you about how a useful idiot can turn into a critical thinker.

Remember when you asked me if an intelligent person could be an idiot in the sense we described, and also if an idiot, as we described it, could turn into a critical thinker?

Well, these are perfect examples of highly intelligent individuals who, at some moment in their lives, hadn't understood their condition as useful idiots within a system. However, upon making use of the method we described, that is, by analyzing in depth the purpose of what they were doing, they radically changed their lives, considering their existence had to be based on being rather than having.

C. What's the difference between living on being rather than having?

P. The difference lies in the fact that you prioritize what you want to be, instead of what you want to have.

Snowden could enjoy a very well-paid job in Hawaii, yet he put his life at stake to follow his conscience. Wylie refused a doubled salary from his employer and also left his job, with no future in sight. Haugen and Bejar found themselves facing a similar dilemma: continue to enjoy a stable and well-paid job, or jeopardize it, for the sole purpose of benefiting the public?

A great book by Erich Fromm entitled "To Have or to Be?" published in 1976, sets the terms of the problem.

Our whistleblowers faced the question: have financial success and the reputation of working in a key role of an important company, or trash it all, for the sole purpose of helping others, by trying to protect them from the invisible threats of the online world?

C. They exercised their critical thinking to the benefit of others.

P. Yes, indeed. Interestingly, our whistleblowers bring to life two fundamental religious intents, which appear to be lost in our technological world.

C. So far, you never highlighted a religious nature in them.

P. True, it's not something they openly display. However, considering how they steered their lives toward a new goal, I noticed two intents which are present in a Christian soul.

The first is confession.

C. You mean confession of sins, just like in church?

P. Yes, even if not quite like in church, the dynamic is the same.

This is very clear in Snowden's book "Permanent Record", in Wylie's book "Mindf*ck. Cambridge Analytica and the Plot to Break America", and in Haugen's book "The Power of One".

All these books are outright confessions.

In each case, it's about someone who deeply repents the sin of having betrayed the people, by being part of that restricted group who, behind the scenes, manipulates billions of online users.

With one difference, however. The repentant Catholic Christian relies on a priest as the intermediary in the communication with God.

In the case of our whistleblowers, they reach out directly to the public to confess their wrongdoings and atone for their sins by revealing the truth.

C. How about the other whistleblowers you mentioned?

P. The difference is only in form, not in substance. Even if other whistleblowers may not have written books describing their journey in undertaking their deed, they went through other ways such as interviews with the press, online podcasts and shows, or in Congress hearings.

In this respect, Tristan Harris reached his own state of enlightenment even sooner, as opposed to the others we mentioned, who dwelled for a longer time within those dark corporations.

Paradoxically, even if all these types of confession don't have the hallmarks of a religious attitude, their ethical message reaches out to a far wider audience than a one-to-one confession in church.

Remember when we talked about the collective power of critical thinking? In the case of whistleblowers, we see them taking action to benefit the freedom of millions, if not billions, of people.

C. You mentioned there's a second intent apart from confession.

P. Yes, the second intent is actually at the root of confession, it precedes it.

I express it through a quote from the Gospel of John: "The truth shall make you free".

Just as simple as it sounds, it's an extremely powerful statement. Before turning into whistleblowers, what were these people seeking in the depth of their heart?

C. They were seeking a truthful existence, as opposed to the fakeness of the roles they had before changing the course of their lives.

P. This is precisely the nature of the problem we started talking about. The problem of living a fake life where you aren't the person in charge of yourself, when you either manipulate others, or let yourself be manipulated.

Our whistleblowers identified with clarity the nature of this problem and sought the logical solution of breaking away from the system, informing as many other people they could about their being manipulated, thus proving what I mentioned earlier about the collective power of critical thinking. A single individual can bring awareness to a group of other individuals. When doing so, an individual process like critical thinking becomes a collective process to the benefit of all.

This idea is perfectly summarized in the title of Frances Haugen's book which reads: "The Power of One".

It's amazing to see how much one individual can help develop critical thinking in many others.

C. If that's the case, what changes occurred in the world after their revelations?

P. I'll start with the bad news: there is no evidence so far of a radical change within those organizations, whether we refer to state-owned entities or social media companies, who are accountable for their intrusive and manipulative activities.

However, the good news is that the revelations from our whistleblowers certainly increased the awareness of people about being used as useful idiots. This has triggered debates on a global scale, mostly in countries where free speech is allowed. In those same countries, generically named democracies, political authorities have asked a few of our whistleblowers to testify before them.

In the last few years, some of our whistleblowers testified on several occasions before the U.S. Congress and the European Parliament. Members of Congress and of the European Parliament have been working on new laws aided by the contributions of whistleblowers.

More specifically, the European Union approved two groups of regulations which came into effect in 2022: the Digital Markets Act (DMA) and the Digital Services Act (DSA). The former addresses the abuse of market power by large online platforms. The latter addresses the way online platforms interact with users, requiring transparency in the use of algorithms, how advertising is managed, illegal content and so forth.

On the U.S. side, after revising several bills finalized at protecting young online users, Congress is yet to approve KOSA, the Kids Online Safety Act. It actually passed the Senate in July 2024, but yet has to pass the House of Representatives.

C.Will these laws effectively prevent online control and manipulation?

P.In first place, we must consider the revolution we are living through, as I described it earlier.

In the last couple of decades, the world has seen the extremely fast development of the internet and internet-capable devices, such as today's phones.

This extremely fast technological development had a massive impact on society. Society as a whole radically changed and is rapidly changing, as we speak. Technology has transformed the way people and companies interact.

It's therefore not surprising to acknowledge how politics has lagged behind, versus the swift and radical changes occurred within society, brought about by technology.

As a result, legislative activity lags behind as well, when addressing these changes.

By the way, it also took some time before laws enforcing seat belts in cars and laws against smoking were enacted.

C. Do you believe it may be just a matter of time before laws will be enacted in order to protect online users?

P. I'm not too optimistic about political authorities acting independently on these wide-ranging developments of technology. This is proven by the fact that if the whistleblowers we talked about hadn't uncovered the manipulative systems adopted by large online entities and corporations, it's unlikely political authorities such as Congress would have started taking steps against such systems.

The whole purpose of our present conversation is to involve as many people as possible in order to create a movement pushing for the necessary changes, starting from the population and directed to the political authorities.

C. I seem to understand you would like the surge for change to originate from the exploited online users, rather than from the restricted elite of whistleblowers, as it happened so far.

P. That is so, even if manipulative techniques are invisible to our senses, because we need to exert an intellective effort in order to identify them and take action accordingly.

However, it's not just about the invisible and stealthy ways which allow manipulative social control from top to bottom, where you have the big tech structures at the top and the people at the bottom. This control is possible thanks to the limited use people make of critical thinking.

In the first part of our conversation, I had explained to you how critical thinking isn't a quality which is proportionate to one's intelligence. It obviously requires intellective effort, therefore intelligence, however the will to retain individual freedom must sustain the use of intelligence which determines critical thinking.

C. You're implying whistleblowers don't have the greater success they deserve, not because people don't grasp the nature of control and manipulation as whistleblowers describe them, but because people don't seem to be really motivated to protect their individual freedom. This motivation is at the core of critical thinking.

P. I'm pleased to acknowledge how you're getting ahead of me, since we first started our conversation.

Let me give you one more hint to prove the crucial role of motivation in critical thinking. The moment people perceive a threat to their financial status, even if this threat may be invisible to their senses, they exert a considerable amount of intellective effort to protect themselves accordingly. How many times have you noticed people who appear to be dumb, display instead extraordinary sharpness in pinning down some apparently minor details which affect their financial situation?

C. That is definitely true. Money is a great driver.

P. Right. So, this means people can incredibly raise their alertness when money is involved. My ambition is to trigger that same alertness when control and manipulation are carried out against their individual freedom. This is what our conversation is all about.

Social Media

P. I described the nature of the revolution we're living in, with the internet and phones taking over a significant amount of our daily activity.

Our phones and apps aren't simply a new way for us to communicate and socialize. They are themselves a third party who's actively participating in our social environment.

C. What do you exactly mean by this?

P. The phone and apps we use to connect with other people aren't simple conduits carrying our communications. They play a very active role, just like as if they were an actor themselves. A comparison with how people socialized in the past, will help to better understand what I'm saying.

Up to just over a couple of decades ago, before the internet came around with smartphones replacing the old ordinary cell phones, people would socialize and communicate mostly in person. Nothing like what's going on now, with people watching and checking their phones for hours during the day.

C. You said the phone is like a third party who's actively taking part in our communications.

P. Yes, I'm getting at it. Today's online platforms referred to as social media, aren't only a new revolutionary means of communication. They also play an active role in shaping the way we communicate and socialize. I'll give you some names of online platforms known as social media, which count billions or hundreds of millions of users: Facebook, Instagram, TikTok, YouTube, Linkedin, X, Pinterest, Snapchat.

This follows from what I had previously explained about how phones work, how they're designed to control and manipulate our actions by continuously collecting data. Once this data is collected, it's used to manipulate us.

C. How do those platforms actually manipulate us?

P. I'll take a surreal approach in order to reply to your question.

C. Surreal? Are you kidding me?

P. It's actually so real that it becomes surreal. What I mean is that reality often exceeds fiction. This is one of those cases. We're led to think we must use our imagination to think about the most incredible stories. We then read newspapers and come across real situations which have the hallmarks of absurdity, to a point of appearing invented, but the sad thing is, they are absolutely real.

C. What would be so absurd about social media?

P. Remember when just a few minutes ago I told you about whistleblowers testifying before Congress?

C. I sure do.

P. Well, those Congress hearings portray surreal or absurd situations almost like a theatre play by Samuel Beckett. During the last few years there have been many hearings in Congress. Different groups have attended those hearings.

Those groups can be summarized as follows: a group which includes whistleblowers and academics, one which includes members of Congress, one which includes executives of social media companies, and one which includes victims and family members of victims of social media.

Depending on the hearing we select, we may find more than two of these groups to be present at the same time.

C. Why do you compare these hearings to theatre plays?

P. I compare them to theatre plays for several reasons. In first place, each group is like a character, because regardless of the fact you have different individuals within each group, they display a similar stance within the same group.

As our first group, we consider whistleblowers and academics, who explain in detail the nefarious effects of social media, especially on kids and teens.

The second group consists of members of Congress. They have an inquisitive stance. It can be summarized as follows: is social media causing social and mental health damage? If so, why? What laws should we pass to prevent this from happening?

The third group consists of social media executives who portray a vision which essentially contradicts the whistleblowers' point of view.

The fourth group consists of victims and family members of victims of social media. Their presence alone is a statement against the destructive effects of social media on young people, most notably kids and teens.

C. The simple fact of having different groups displaying different characters makes you believe these Congress hearings are like theatre performances?

P. Not just that, there's more to it. I was referring to a surreal experience, as conveyed by the sense of absurdity of certain theatre plays.

The first condition which generates this sense of absurdity or lack of meaning, is the deep contradiction between the statements from two of these groups, namely the whistleblowers versus the corporate executives of social media companies.

On the one hand, you have the whistleblowers documenting in great detail the nefarious and manipulative methods adopted by social media companies.

On the other hand, you have social media executives underplaying those criticisms and providing assurance over those matters being addressed and taken care of.

I'll soon get into the details of this, but just to give you a rough idea of this kind of situation, it's like as if you were at the hospital close to a patient whose vital signs indicate the patient will likely die in a matter of hours.

On the one hand, you have a doctor, say our whistleblower, claiming the patient is about to die, on the basis of an unquestionable diagnosis.

On the other hand, you have another doctor, our social media executive, who claims the opposite, that is, the patient has some minor health issues, but those are taken care of, and the patient's life isn't in danger at all, so nothing to be worried about.

C. This contradiction leaves you without a clue over who's right or wrong.

P. Not only. The moment you focus on the aftermath of these hearings, you expect some decisive resolution to be taken by Congress, in the light of the serious issues at stake.

The lack of decisive resolutions following those many hearings, today, several years after they took place, furthermore increases my disorientation.

No significant changes regulating the social media industry are yet to be seen. Therefore, in hindsight, all those Congress hearings appear as "flatus vocis", a Latin expression which literally stands for "breath of the voice", implying a disconnect between words and reality.

A surreal situation where all we are left with, is the memory of the mere sound of words.

C. How can it be so? If platforms counting billions of users are proven to have negative effects on those users, they should be held accountable, and all the appropriate countermeasures should be taken.

P. Yes, disappointed expectations make this state of things even more surreal. However, even if you understood my idea about who's right and who's wrong, I'll now start telling you the arguments of our whistleblowers, and I will be very happy if you'll take more time to go deeper into the matter, so that you reach some conclusions on your own, by making the best possible use of your critical thinking.

C. By what I understood so far, you seem to be standing all on the whistleblowers' side, and against the social media executives.

P. You're absolutely right on this. However, you'll remember I explained how you should never take any opinion for good until you analyze it by using critical thinking. I'll be very glad to hear any objections of yours to my conclusions.

C. What is so bad about social media?

P. As a starting point, I'll take a Congress hearing held on January 8, 2020 in the House of Representatives.
On that occasion, well-documented information was provided in reply to your question asking what is so bad about social media.

When listening to that hearing, and reading the documents provided at the time of the hearing, I felt like a dwarf standing on the shoulders of a giant, where, in this case, the giant of critical thinking was Tristan Harris.

I'm borrowing this expression from the Christian philosopher Bernard of Chartres who lived in the twelfth century. He considered himself as a dwarf standing on the shoulders of giants, who were the ancient scholars of Greece and Rome. This means we can see more and farther thanks to the gigantic stature of our predecessors.

By the way, I'll never forget my visit to the Cathedral of Chartres, in France. I still carry in me that magnificent sense of beauty and mystical fascination.

C. I have to assume Tristan Harris' statements had an enlightening effect on you.

P. It is definitely so, altogether with his work at the Center of Humane Technology, as I mentioned to you earlier.

In Congress, he had the difficult task of explaining in a plain way technical concepts which the members of Congress weren't quite familiar with.

C. What were these concepts?

P. In first place, I strongly invite you to follow that Congress hearing I mentioned. You find the video and transcripts of that hearing on the U.S. Congress website, as well as videos of it on YouTube.

I'll give you a brief selection of some sharp quotes by Tristan Harris.

These quotes are from his January 2020 testimony:

"How much have you paid for your Facebook account recently, or your YouTube account? Zero. How are they worth more than a trillion dollars in market value? They monetize our attention. The way they get that attention is by influencing you, and using the dark patterns or tricks to do it."

"We have a supercomputer pointed at your brain, meaning like the Facebook news feed sitting there, and using the vast resources of 2.7 billion people's behavior to calculate the perfect thing to show you next."

"It knows more about your weaknesses than you know about yourself, and the degree of asymmetry is far beyond anything we have experienced."

"It is as if a psychotherapist who knows everything about your weaknesses, uses it with a for-profit advertising business model."

C. What does he exactly mean when he says "the degree of asymmetry is far beyond anything we have experienced"?

P. He means what I had started explaining to you about phones using you, rather than you using them. The asymmetry he's referring to, is the difference between the huge power companies behind phones and apps have over users, and, on the opposite end, the lack of power the users are left with.

C. Let me get this straight. Tristan Harris is saying that when you're active on social media, say Facebook, everything you do there is recorded, so to create a profile of who you are. This way, you receive the most appropriate ads and news feeds.

What's so bad about this?

P. It's extremely bad. You'll see it the moment you'll understand exactly how this works, and I'll explain the matter in greater detail for you to realize why I'm saying so.

Among the available documents pertaining to that same Congress hearing of January 8, 2020, there are two very important ones with writings from Tristan Harris. Reading these two documents alone, is like reading a book which explains why I'm telling you the current situation is extremely bad. You can download both documents from the Congress website.

 The first document is a 10-page PDF file entitled "Additional Questions for the Record". The second is a 19-page PDF file which contains a written statement prepared for this specific hearing.

Both documents are a must-read. Tristan Harris provides a very clear and insightful picture of how the manipulation of billions of users is carried out by social media companies. The documents contain a useful summary of the apparently innocuous features which actually manipulate users into addiction.

C. I'll read them, but I'd also like you to provide more detailed explanations, so I can better understand the negative effects of social media.

P. Before doing so, I want to remember that in that same January 2020 hearing, Facebook executive Monika Bickert provided her testimony. When listening to her, I found myself thrown into that surreal environment I was telling you about.

The setting of the hearing was like a glorification of nonsense. By this I don't mean the two parties involved, Tristan Harris on one side, and Monika Bickert on the other, were talking nonsense.

The point is they were supposed to speak about the same subject matter, that is, the reasons of the harms caused by those social media platforms.

However, they were conceiving them and addressing them in totally different ways. Tristan Harris focused on the intrinsic, structural features of the business model of the platforms as the root cause of the problem. Bickert focused on how to keep the bad guys off the platforms, essentially diverting the negative factors onto the users.

A surreal situation were those two parties are each given time to express their thoughts, on equal grounds, but their respective focus happens to be centered on totally different priorities.

C. What is specifically surreal in this case?

P. It's the fact that they're supposed to address the same issue, but they explain it in totally different ways.

Following a metaphor which is similar to one used by Tristan Harris, it's like as if the security features of a nuclear power plant fail, and radiations spread across the population. In this scenario, the whistleblowers point to the failed security systems as the root cause of the catastrophe, while the social media executives blame the victims for not having protected themselves with appropriate protective suits, regardless of this being totally useless for the purpose.

C. So, what those executives are saying is: our system isn't intrinsically harmful, it's just about some bad users who may get involved.

P. It is essentially so. Along these lines, the discussion is headed to nowhere, obviously because one side is concealing the truth and misplaces the nature of the problem.

This brought to my mind a ludicrous statement by the founder of Facebook, Mark Zuckerberg, who had claimed Facebook was designed to bring people together, portraying the idea of creating a happy online world.

The worst part of this, is the deep hypocrisy of these executives who are perfectly aware of their manipulative techniques and their negative effects on the mental health of millions of young people, as whistleblowers like Frances Haugen and Arturo Bejar have clearly shown, by publishing internal company records proving the awareness of those executives about this state of things.

C. I want to better understand the reasons of this hypocrisy.

P. The idea according to which social media are designed to bring people together, thus exercising a social function, is a gigantic scam encompassing our planet. Only a sheer idiot can believe this.

You'll find evidence of this in the two documents by Tristan Harris, I just referred you to.

Social media work exclusively on the basis of a business model aimed at increasing engagement as much as possible. Machine learning and algorithms are used by social media in order to keep your eyes stuck to your phone's screen as much as possible, ideally 24/7, regardless of any consequences on your mental health.

This is exactly the opposite of a humane approach, it actually paves the way to alienation, meaning that you get carried away from your real self into a dimension where algorithms change the traits of your personality, without you actually being aware of it.

C. How does this actually work? How can your personality be swayed in such a way?

P. User engagement is one essential condition social media require, in order to make money.

Another essential condition is to create the most accurate profile of each user.

Once these two conditions are satisfied, a company like Meta, which comprises several others, most notably Facebook and Instagram, can basically sell you to the advertisers who pay Meta to display their ads on its platforms. You, as the user of their platforms, are the product sold by those platforms to their customers, the advertisers.

You may recall when I explained to you the difference between the old traditional ads shown on TV where those ads follow a unidirectional flow, without any interaction with the user, versus the bidirectional flow of data on social media platforms.

With social media we have a far more powerful mechanism at play along a bidirectional flow of data where the user, through her screen taps, likes, scrolls, choices, contacts and so on, provides a massive wealth of information of herself allowing a very accurate positioning of ads which therefore become far more effective than traditional TV ads which are basically broadcast along a unidirectional flow, with no real-time feedback from the users.

C. How is this user profiling carried out?

P. Considering social media count billions of users, profiling is carried out by algorithms and machine learning models.

In his book "Mindf*ck. Cambridge Analytica and the Plot to Break America", Christopher Wylie, one of the whistleblowers I referred to earlier, reports a 2015 study where a computer model using Facebook likes could predict a person's behavior better than other humans close to that person.

With ten likes from the user, the computer model predicted a person's behavior better than her co-workers. With one hundred and fifty likes, it would predict it better than a family member. With three hundred likes, it would predict it better than that person's spouse.

As Wylie explains, one of the reasons of the accuracy of that computer model, is that it can see all your interactions on the platform. As an example, it can see how wild you can get at 3 AM of the night, while people around you have a partial view of yourself, not to mention all your phone-based activity which is tracked by your screen taps, which nobody around you can follow, unless you have someone behind your shoulder checking your phone activity 24/7, which is a very unlikely scenario.

That computer model can ultimately know your habits better than yourself. It outpaces humans in personality judgement.

C. This sounds scary.

P. It is scary.

We feel we're freely communicating with others on our apps, but our apps silently monitor everything we're doing, our social contents on social media are moderated according to standards which we don't define and which we're forced to accept. The ways we interact with others through our phones are set by people behind the scenes who're in control of our apps, and who direct and manage the ways we can or cannot socialize. Your socializing habits are measured and analyzed. Those same apps are designed and updated to keep you addicted to them as much as possible.

The logic of major social media apps doesn't allow you to question this socializing model. You have to accept it, whether you like it or not. Far from being a conduit, social media are an invasive presence which modify the way we relate ourselves to others and to the world.

C. In what ways do social media apps exert control over their users?

P. The moment you become a user of a social media app, the companies behind those apps collect data about you. Their goal is to have the most accurate profile of your personality, your social and political preferences and so on. This is where monitoring does its job through data collection.

Individual profiles of billions of users are stored by tech companies which have their software installed on your phone. You become a number in a massive database. That information is used by those companies or by business partners of those same companies, to direct your attention to certain topics or products you're likely to be interested in. This is where control supersedes collection of private and personal information. You're not aware you're fed certain news or products which you haven't chosen yourself upfront.

The moment you're influenced by that news or ad, the step from being analyzed and monitored, to being controlled, is complete. You naively believe you're the one in control of your decisions, but you're not, because your decisions, for example deciding to buy a certain product, are the result of your being manipulated.

Don't forget that ads are in most cases the main source of revenue of social media apps.

C. You're describing a process of manipulation which hides itself behind the idea of getting people together.

P. Correct. The deepest level of hypocrisy is how social media portray themselves as platforms which favor socialization, that is, bringing people together, while they are instead structured to achieve the exact opposite.

"Psychographic micro-targeting" is one of the magical formulas which ultimately produce segregation instead of socialization.

The term "psychographic" is derived from psychographics which, in the realm of social media, is a discipline focused on identifying psychological attributes of individuals on the basis of their online behavior and personal data. It goes without saying that private information of individuals is the material which is subject to psychographic analysis.

"Micro-targeting" is the work of collecting large amounts of online data of individuals, where all this data is analyzed in order to create and convey messages that reflect the preferences of those individuals, so to influence their behavior. This entails the segmentation of individuals into groups.

C. All this jargon sounds like engineering. Where's the human factor?

P. Great question. The answer is: nowhere.

Algorithms are developed in order to make your behavior more pronounced in certain traits which define you as being part of the group the system has assigned to you. Targeted ads and news are thrown at you, so that you can become even more entrenched within the group the system has assigned you to. All this creates gated communities, rather than one free open community.

It's the exact opposite of Zuckerberg's founding statement about bringing people together.

Algorithms are structured in order to increase the engagement of single users. More engagement entails more time spent on your phone, more time on your phone means more time to serve you ads and content structured to do, guess what? Engage you even more.

Engagement brings addiction. There you go: once you're addicted, you're a full-fledged useful idiot.

C. All this means social media users are victims of sophisticated and highly automated social engineering. If that is so, it is, as you say, a gigantic scam.

P. Yes, where your personal information, which is your property, is used in order to serve the strategies of who is behind that social media platform, regardless of whatever legal jargon is studied to have your consent about the terms of that platform.

C. Which begs the question whether social media improve the quality of your life.

P. An indication that social media, contrary to what they claim, aren't designed to improve your social life, is the emotional damage to people who are addicted to their use. The rise in use of phones and social media goes hand in hand with the rise of depression and anxiety among its users. Many studies have shown these correlations. Studies have also proven how addiction and lack of attention are associated to phone usage. By lack of attention, I mean a strong degradation of focus on healthy and useful daily activities, as well as reduced learning capacity at school.

C. Where can I find information about mental health damage caused by phone addiction?

P. As a starter, I'll provide you with two resources, which will lead you to additional resources and documentation.

The first is the website www.humanetech.com, managed by Tristan Harris. You'll remember I had already suggested it as must-go-to in the previous part of our conversation.

The second is the website www.anxiousgeneration.com.

The name of this website follows the title of an enlightening book: "The Anxious Generation" by Jonathan Haidt, a social psychologist at New York University's Stern School of Business.

The author proves how mental illness, depression and anxiety have greatly increased in teens after 2010, in conjunction with a similar increase in phone and social media usage. He highlights a specific time frame of five years between 2010 and 2015 when what he calls "the great rewiring of childhood" took place.

In the light of these findings, the author strongly supports the following four counteractions to be taken at a general level: no phones (intended as smartphones) before high school, no social media before the age of sixteen, phone-free schools (including any other text-capable devices), more unsupervised play and childhood independence. The latter allows to naturally develop social skills.

C. You imply that rather than a progress in the way people socialize, social media have brought about a regression. Is this because we now socialize through media which control our interactions without us being aware of it?

P. Lack of awareness is precisely the problem. The moment we become aware of the manipulative socializing model we adhere to, we can start to question it.

I'll throw another red flag at you, which hopefully will raise your awareness furthermore: we know that people who work or have worked in social media companies, are very careful before allowing the use of phones to their own young children. This means that such people perfectly understand how being stuck on a phone for hours generates mental damage.

Speaking of people holding important positions within social media companies, two whistleblowers we dwelled upon earlier, that is, Frances Haugen and Arturo Bejar, also testified before Congress, respectively in 2021 and 2023.

I had already mentioned this to you, but I want to highlight once more that both whistleblowers divulged internal documents proving how the top management of Meta, encompassing Facebook and Instagram, was perfectly aware of the mental health damage caused by those platforms on millions of kids and teens, yet took no effective countermeasure.

The documents are there, proving the full awareness of Meta's executives about the mental health damage on kids and teens. When summoned on the matter by members of Congress, we find our typical social media executive downplaying the importance of the questions and throwing us back again into that surreal atmosphere I described, where the mere sound of words echoes across the air of those solemn hearings.

C. Once again we have to thank whistleblowers for allowing us to understand what's going on behind the scenes.

P. It is definitely so. We wouldn't have the knowledge of the deep threats of the online world, without the contributions of whistleblowers. Mind you, this isn't at all about cybercrime, like scams carried out through spam emails, identity theft and so forth. In this respect, the online world also carries its load of crime, just like it is present in our life offline.

The threat revealed by our whistleblowers is deeper and more dangerous than cybercrime, because it stems from sources which are considered perfectly legitimate and have far wider reach than cybercrime itself.

C. This shows how critical thinking must be driven by an ethical intent. In other words, it has to be sustained by the desire of remaining free individuals.

P. That is precisely so. This is proven by how the top executives of those companies where our whistleblowers worked, are totally numb to the idea of subordinating critical thinking to individual freedom.

This goes back to what I was mentioning to you earlier, about the hypocrisy of the top executives of such companies, making sure not to have their children stuck onto their phones in order to spare them the brain damage which, however, their own platforms are very happy to inflict on other people's children.

C. It's everywhere for you to see: obsessively checking social media is almost a way of life for many people.

P. It is, because they have been manipulated into it, like following trends in the fashion industry. The way people dress, often reflects the same sheep-effect which forces people into social media.

I'll give you an example: if you wore ripped jeans sixty years ago, people would look at you like a lunatic, but if you do it today you're cool. Just as social media trends, the fashion industry creates trends which people follow. Dressing up in a trendy way reflects the idea that someone else decides what's nice for you.

Let's play a short conversation game now, so I can prove my point. I'm the guy wearing ripped jeans, and you have to ask me why I'm doing so. Don't just ask me the question once, insist with me until you receive a satisfactory answer and try to challenge me over a valid reason for wearing ripped jeans, okay?

C. Okay. Why are you wearing those ripped jeans?

P. I'm wearing them because I see many people around me are wearing them.

C. You like those jeans simply because many people around you are wearing them?

P. Correct, I noticed many people around me were wearing them, so I got to like them.

C. Therefore, you're proving my point which is: you get to like something just because people around you appear to be liking it.

P. You expressed it perfectly. I like to wear something because I feel comfortable about many people around me wearing the same. Would nobody around me be wearing it, I'd feel awkward.

C. This shows how many of us seek the approval of others, so we tend to adjust our behavior and habits following people around us, without asking ourselves if it's the best thing for us to do.

P. Yes, by doing so, we sacrifice our own opinion of ourselves in favor of the opinion of others about ourselves, but as a free thinker, I shouldn't behave guided by how others will judge my behavior. This would go against my dignity as an individual.

Let me bring up another example which is a tragic one but conveys the same idea underlying the case of our ripped jeans.

C. Tragic?

P. Yes, it's an extreme case, but also a true story.

I once knew an artist whose great production of art works wasn't successful. I liked his art works and thought they were better than those of many other successful artists of his time. When talking to him, you had the feeling this guy had a great opinion of his works, however he was facing the frustration of having no success. He entered into a state of depression and eventually killed himself. There may have been several factors at play including some mental health issues, but the single cause he ascribed to his depression was the lack of approval his works found on the market.

There were two conflicting dimensions in his mind.

One was his own internal self-belief which set the grounds for him to think he was a great artist.

The other was his realization of the lack of consideration the world had for his art works.

The dimension of his mind which was forged by the external world, ended up overwhelming his own internal dimension, up to the point of convincing him he was worth nothing.

C. He killed himself because the power of the external world dictated his value.

P. Exactly, and, mind you, the same mechanism is at play when your image in social media replaces your real self, overwhelming it. Depression and suicide rates among teens have increased with the rise of social media, as documented in "The Anxious Generation".

This has affected a considerable number of girls, especially on Instagram, as documented, among others, by Haugen, Bejar and Haidt.

C. It doesn't look like the general population seems to be concerned about these effects of social media.

P. This is because critical thinking isn't widespread among those billions of social media users. Were users aware of the downsides of social media we described, their number would decrease for sure. This is the root of the problem which I tried to stress throughout our entire conversation. Aside from the negative consequences of phone addiction, the real issue at stake is your freedom.

Critical thinking allows a social media user to realize that users are being used by the app, rather than the users using it. As a result, that user starts seeking countermeasures, such as considering to stop using certain apps.

C. But if that user's peers and friends use that same app she wants to stop using, this will imply losing contact with those peers and friends. The user may decide to keep things as is, in order to stay in contact with peers and friends.

P. Unless the user starts telling her peers and friends that she's sick to be a tool in the hands of social media apps and incites her peers and friends to question the quality of their relationship through the app.

C. How would you do that?

P. Say I'm in contact with my friends through social media by obsessively spending hours every day on my phone with them. This is a condition of enslavement where social media run my life.

I want to set a very ambitious goal: free our lives from being exploited by social media. Please don't get me wrong: as I explained earlier, I don't want to eliminate phones and social media. I want to be the one in control of them, not the one controlled by them.

This is the point I want to make clear to my friends. I want all of them to know about the conversation I'm having with you. In other words, I must do everything I can to turn them into critical thinkers.

Solutions

P. We're approaching the end of today's conversation. I started it by telling you how you can become a critical thinker.

Can you now tell me in your own words what is critical thinking, and why is it so important?

C. It's a method which considers with a doubtful mindset any information received. It's a constructive doubt, meaning that I have to approach information in an unbiased way, analyzing it thoroughly, trying to determine its truthfulness, so that I won't be manipulated or used by others. By doing so, I must leverage my reasoning capacity at the best of my efforts. The ultimate result of this method is to achieve freedom of thought and action, as well as the dignity every individual deserves.

P. It's a good summary. Let me just add one more idea which is implicit in what you just said.

Critical thinking is a way of life.

It's not a speculative mind game. It's a quality you should have to mould your life and what you want to do with it. It precedes and sustains your actions. By virtue of this, it's not an intellective quality alone, it's necessarily a moral quality.

After having explained to you the basics of the critical thinking method, I applied it to the use of the two most invasive elements in the lives of today's teens, that is, the phone and social media.

We went through the many ways phones and social media control and manipulate you.

This is a problem.

Of course, it's a problem because we care about our individual freedom. It obviously wouldn't be a problem, if we were okay about living as useful idiots manipulated by others.

Now, let me ask you: what happens when we determine we have a problem?

C. We must find a solution to the problem.

P. That is definitely so. Let me tell you one more thing here. The better you understand the nature of the problem, the better will be your solution to the problem itself.

You will remember I told you about people who, by making use of critical thinking, realized they were facing a problem, namely they understood they were manipulating other people's lives.

C. I do remember. Those people are the whistleblowers you talked about.

Did they also formulate any practical solutions, in order to change this state of things, so to prevent entities or corporations from controlling or manipulating the population?

P. Yes, absolutely. To a lesser or greater extent, all our whistleblowers have been very vocal about radical changes which are necessary in order to move away from this state of things.

These changes can have two different directions: top-to-bottom, versus bottom-to-top.

Top-to-bottom are changes which originate from the political authorities, or the government in general terms, and affect society as a whole, including state-owned entities, online platforms and online users.

Bottom-to-top are changes which originate from the population at large, affecting state-owned entities and online platforms. Bottom-to-top changes may ultimately affect the decisions of the political authorities, who may acknowledge requests for changes from the people and turn those requests into laws.

C. In what way do these two directions of change differ from one another?

P. First off, these two different directions by which changes can take place, are complementary. They mustn't be seen as alternate solutions. On the contrary, they integrate with each other.

The top-to-bottom direction requires the necessary changes to originate from the political authorities.

This means that the political authorities enact laws and rules, which serve the purpose of protecting all citizens from the invasive and manipulative activities of state-owned entities and online platforms, which use technology for those purposes.

C. How about bottom-to-top changes?

P. An example of a possible bottom-to-top change could be our present conversation. By sharing our present conversation with an expanded audience, some of our readers may rethink and change their approach to their online activities.

This would mean that, without having to wait for new laws which restrict the power of entities like the NSA or platforms like Facebook, individual users would become more privacy-conscious and no more exploitable by online platforms.

C. Between top-to-bottom and bottom-to-top changes, which would be more effective?

P. Let's consider for a moment a radical scenario for each of the two types of changes.

Radical top-to-bottom changes would imply a heavy restructuring of entities like the NSA which wouldn't be collecting any more individual records of the population and wouldn't have access to anybody's phone and online activity. By applying the same approach to social media platforms, their inner workings would become fully transparent. Collection of users' personal data would be prohibited.

Algorithms influencing user choices, and any addictive feature, would be banned.

Radical bottom-to-top changes would imply five billion phone users switching to open-source phone operating systems, trashing Android or iOS, thereafter hardening all their privacy settings. At the same time, they would openly boycott all social media platforms, which would be left with no users to offer to their advertisers. In this second scenario, the world population would become a self-regulating entity driven by critical thinking, rather than benefiting from regulations originating from the political authorities.

C. The first top-to-bottom scenario would probably be more plausible, as I can't imagine five billion phone users changing their phone operating systems and openly boycotting social media.

P. This is why our whistleblowers are requesting the political authorities to enact new laws, as they would protect the population of phone users from the abuse of state-owned entities and social media.

However, I'll give you a hint of how difficult it is for minimal changes to even get started, by considering another surreal situation in Congress which I haven't yet told you about.

C. Are you referring to one of those hearings where a whistleblower was confronted with some executive of a social media corporation?

P. Not quite. This time around, it's about a single question and single answer between a U.S. Senator and Mark Zuckerberg, the boss of Facebook, at the U.S. Senate hearing of April 10, 2018, in the wake of the revelations by Christopher Wylie, also referred to as the "Cambridge Analytica scandal".

This moment was rightly highlighted because it represented the most significant few seconds of the entire hearing.

Senator Hatch asked Zuckerberg, amongst other things: "...how do you sustain a business model in which users don't pay for your service?"

Zuckerberg's reply was: "Senator, we run ads".

This moment became so popular, to a point that a domain was even registered, by the name of www.senatorwerunads.com, owned by a company specialized in digital marketing.

C. What's so surreal about this moment of the hearing?

P. What's surreal is the disconnect between the different level of knowledge and awareness of the respective parties.

The candid question by the Senator, in the way it is conveyed, betrays the ignorance of the questioning party about the inner workings of Facebook.

The easy reply by Zuckerberg makes things sound obvious, but actually conceals the intrinsically manipulative way those ads are run.

The point I want to make here, is that, if this is the start of a congressional process finalized at regulating the most invasive social media platform, well, it looks like it's ages behind, before anything gets accomplished.

It would be ludicrous to believe those same platforms will take action to regulate themselves because that would entail the destruction of the business model on which they're founded.

Therefore, it's up to the political authorities to enforce regulations aimed at controlling and stopping the nefarious effects of technology.

C. How would those regulations look like?

P. We should draw a distinction about the entities which need to be regulated.

In the case of state-owned entities, Snowden proved their granular intrusiveness on the population. Those entities need to be regulated and controlled, following the idea that they should be at the service of the people, and not the other way round.

Snowden clearly explained how the NSA performed an ongoing granular collection of all possible private data of citizens through their phones and their online activity. What has to be done here isn't complicated: it has to stop. No more mass surveillance. Period.

In the case of online platforms such as social media companies, they must be made accountable for the way information is handled on their platforms and made liable for the mental health damage to their users.

Following my explanations on the inner workings of social media platforms, it goes without saying that any effective regulation would heavily impact the business model on which they are founded.

C. New laws must be enacted on state-owned entities and online platforms in order to safeguard the privacy and freedom of the people.

P. Yes, and our whistleblowers have indicated the way to follow.

Going back to what we said earlier, the deep knowledge of a problem is the start for finding a good solution to the problem itself.

C. What's the right course of action, according to our whistleblowers?

P. In first place, by raising awareness in the population through their revelations, they paved the way for bottom-to-top solutions, which are solutions generated from the population and directed against the intrusiveness of state-owned entities and online platforms.

I'm not implying people should take the radical stance of Richard Stallman who lives without a phone, so he can't be tracked, as I had mentioned to you earlier in our conversation.

However, there are many other actions people can take to change things bottom-to-top, as I mentioned, such as hardening phone privacy settings and boycotting social media.

These are all measures our whistleblowers would welcome.

C. How about top-to-bottom solutions advocated by whistleblowers?

P. You'll find many ideas in their writings and public interviews.

One reference is the 10-page PDF file entitled "Additional Questions for the Record" related to Tristan Harris' Congress testimony on January 8, 2020, where he replies to questions about what changes should take place.

More ideas on the matter are in the final chapter named "Epilogue: On Regulation: A Note to Legislators" of Christopher Wylie's book I had mentioned to you in the previous part of our conversation.

Along the same lines, you'll find more suggestions in the final chapter named "Onward and Upward" of Frances Haugen's book I had also brought up earlier.

Not to forget the proposals I had described to you, advanced by social psychologist Jonathan Haidt, about limiting the use of phones, especially among teens.

C. If you were to sum up these top-to-bottom changes advocated by our whistleblowers, how would you describe them?

P. With specific reference to social media platforms, the keyword is "regulation", to be implemented through laws and guidelines which will necessarily restrict the huge power of those platforms.

These laws will be aimed at making these platforms accountable for their activities and for the damage they cause, specifically to teens like you, as I described in the previous part of our conversation.

Not only: new rules will have to regulate the inner workings of the platforms which will have to lift their veil of secrecy.

C. How can that be achieved on social media?

P. In various ways.

Controls will be needed to prevent the mechanisms of manipulation we described, amongst other things, by imposing audits to be carried out by third parties which include academics or researchers who have the required competence to evaluate those inner workings.

New digital regulatory agencies would be established. These would audit the inner workings of platforms, imposing transparency.

As an example, just like the FAA carries out controls on aircraft safety, by the same token those regulatory agencies should make sure the standards set by law are followed, punishing any deviation from those standards.

The safety and privacy of all online users must be at the heart of these regulations.

Wylie also sets forth the interesting idea of enforcing a professional code of conduct for software engineers. Just like doctors, nurses, lawyers, teachers, architects, engineers must follow certain standards in order to guarantee the safety of the people affected by their activity, so should software engineers be bound by standards oriented to that purpose.

C. I'd be inclined to believe that, if these laws and regulations were to be applied, they would kill the business model of social media platforms as we see them now.

P. Yes, they would. This explains why it's not an easy task for the political authorities to carry out those changes. They would affect very powerful and profitable corporations who would dedicate their resources to combating such changes.

Under different circumstances, the same difficulties of regulating online platforms would also apply to state-owned entities like the NSA.

C. Have there been any changes in this respect?

P.Speaking of state-owned entities like the NSA, we have good reason to believe no substantial changes have affected the NSA since the revelations of Snowden in 2013.

I'm saying this because we haven't seen regulations effectively impacting the NSA. In other words, we haven't seen any significant legislative action providing the changes advocated by Snowden.

For sure, Snowden's revelations have had a great bottom-to-top impact, meaning that since 2013, the world population is now far more aware of the extremely intrusive power of state-owned entities, through the use, or better said, misuse and abuse of technology. Awareness is the basic condition allowing any bottom-to-top initiative to take shape.

C.How about changes affecting social media platforms?

P.As far as those platforms are concerned, I mentioned to you some legislative steps taken by the European Parliament with the Digital Markets Act and Digital Services Act of 2022, as well as the currently delayed implementation of similar laws by the U.S. Congress.

The bad news is that all the regulatory changes advocated by our whistleblowers are yet to be seen in terms of decisive changes. The question is whether the political authorities will eventually turn them into law and enforce them.

The extremely fast development of the internet and phones, with all their negative side-effects, has certainly caught political institutions by surprise. The current problems carried by social media were almost non-existent two decades ago.

C. This means we yet have to see effective restrictions on those areas of the online world which control and manipulate people's lives.

P. That is so, which makes our present conversation even more important.

With specific reference to social media, by sharing our conversation with others, more and more people will raise their awareness about being useful idiots and will start pulling away from those platforms which dominate their lives.

C. Instead of having changes happening top-to-bottom, that is, from the political authorities to the online world, we would need a revolution taking place bottom-to-top, where citizens start rethinking their relationship with the online world and take action against their exploitation as useful idiots.

P. I couldn't have said it any better.

I'm proud of how you have taken seriously all the matters we discussed.

If the readers of our conversation will take it just as seriously, we'll have succeeded in supporting the cause of our whistleblowers, empowering people to take ownership of their individual freedom through critical thinking.

Giving one last thought to social media, stop and consider for a moment how many hours in a day or in a week you have remained stuck to your phone's screen. Be honest to yourself, and question whether you're addicted to that activity.

If that's the case, consider what we explained in the course of our conversation: you have a supercomputer pointed at your brain, algorithms collect every single activity you carry out on your phone and weaponize it against you in order to enhance your addiction.

If you find yourself addicted, that system has succeeded in turning you into a useful idiot. You lost your critical thinking. You lost your individual freedom. Does this make you feel happy?

I'll leave the answer up to you.

www.ingramcontent.com/pod-product-compliance
Lightning Source LLC
Chambersburg PA
CBHW071221090426
42736CB00014B/2928